CAPITALISM
HITS THE FAN

The Global Economic Meltdown and What to Do About It

Richard D. Wolff

OLIVE
BRANCH
PRESS

An imprint of Interlink Publishing Group, Inc.
www.interlinkbooks.com

This edition first published in 2013 by

OLIVE BRANCH PRESS
An imprint of Interlink Publishing Group, Inc.
46 Crosby Street, Northampton, Massachusetts 01060
www.interlinkbooks.com

Library of Congress Cataloging-in-Publication Data
Wolff, Richard D.
Capitalism hits the fan : the global economic meltdown and what to do about it /
by Richard Wolff.—1st American ed.
p. cm.
Includes index.
ISBN 978-1-56656-936-1 (pbk.)
1. Financial crises—United States—History—21st century. 2. Capitalism—United
States—History—21st century. 3. United States—Economic policy—2001–
I. Title.
HB3722.W64 2009
330.973—dc22
2009025488

Cover image © Littlemacproductions/dreamstime.com

Printed and bound in the United States of America

To request our complete 48-page full-color catalog, please call us toll free at 1-800-238-
LINK, visit our website at www.interlinkbooks.com or write Interlink Publishing, 46
Crosby Street, Northampton, MA 01060
e-mail: info@interlinkbooks.com

Part III: Politics of the Crisis

INTRODUCTION TO SECOND EDITION

This book's first edition was published in late 2009 after two years of deep recession. It explained how and why capitalism was generally crisis-prone and why the current crisis was so deep. It rejected the glib assurances that the US economy would quickly bounce back and resume rapid economic growth. Because other analyses downplayed or ignored the systemic roots of this crisis, the book emphasized them. The capitalist *system* was a major cause of the crisis. That system was likewise deeply influential in shaping how most politicians, journalists, and academics understood the crisis and proposed "solutions" for it.

From the 2013 vantage point of this second edition, we can expand and update our analysis. We can explain how those solutions met the needs of the capitalist system's dominant minority but failed everyone else. Government-run and -funded bailouts of major banks, large corporations, and the stock markets brought some measure of "recovery" for those entities. Republicans and Democrats had agreed on those costly bailouts and on borrowing (hence deficits) to finance them. Meanwhile, economic conditions for most people kept deteriorating— and continue to do so. The endlessly hyped recovery excludes the majority. That exclusion too is a strong tendency within capitalism as a system.

Austerity Policies

We can now also understand why *austerity* (various combinations of tax increases and government spending cuts) was the consensus policy choice agreed upon and endorsed by most Republicans and Democrats after 2010. By then, with "recovery" underway *for them*, large private capitalist interests wanted to ensure that (1) they did not have to pay the costs of those bailouts through higher taxes, (2) crisis-heightened government economic intervention and power were reduced back to pre-crisis levels, and (3) creditors of the US government were secure in their sharply increased holdings of US debt. Austerity was the perfect "policy response" *for them*; it achieved just those three objectives. However, in the United States, unlike in Europe, the dominant discourse prefers more positive language than "austerity."

In the United States, austerity is repackaged as "deficit reduction programs" or "fiscal responsibility," words leaders find more comforting. Distractions such as "fiscal cliffs" and "debt ceilings" serve nicely to focus attention on struggles over the disputed secondary details of austerity rather than on austerity itself. US politicians, media, and academics mostly struggle over whose taxes will go up and how much, and which recipients of government spending will suffer what size cuts. They do not debate austerity itself, the very idea of raising mass taxes and cutting spending on social programs in the midst of a deep recession. They do not explore the interests served and undermined by *any* such austerity policy. So we shall do so here.

Proponents of austerity programs justify them by insistently defining the dominant economic problem today to be overcoming government budgetary imbalance (i.e., taxes raised are less than government spending). This definition removes from discussion *why* that imbalance occurred (i.e., the crisis plus bailouts accelerated budget imbalances in almost all countries). The goal becomes to reduce the imbalance and indeed *not* to focus on what caused it. That avoids the risk of the following logic establishing itself in the popular consciousness: if capitalism causes crises that cause government budget imbalances, then one solution would be to change from capitalism to some other economic system not characterized by recurring crises. Preventing that logic from shaping popular common sense is particularly important to those who created the crisis and secured the bailouts for themselves.

Austerity proponents insist they are meeting what "the market" demands. By such convenient references to an anonymous market of government creditors, they can avoid identifying those creditors. We may assist here: major public creditors of the United States include large banks, insurance companies, major corporations, wealthy individuals, and central banks around the world. Austerity is meant to satisfy "the market" and thereby sustain the credit rating of the United States so that creditors will not require higher interest rates to hold US debt. Rising interest rates would, after all, undermine the "recovery." Such is the economic spin on which austerity policies stand.

Austerity is thus the policy preferred by the private capitalist interests who caused the crisis and took the subsequent bailouts. Those interests now threaten to extract higher interest rates or to withhold credit unless the government that just bailed them out imposes higher taxes (on others) and reduces spending (on others) to lower its budgetary imbalances. Because serious debate and criticism of capitalism had been silenced in the United States since the end of World War II, the leaders imposing austerity in the current deep capitalist crisis imagined little risk of effective mass opposition.

The Keynesian critics of austerity have enjoyed pointing out that the United States has been able to borrow limitlessly at historically low interest rates through this crisis. Thus no real problem of troubling "the market" actually exists. The Keynesians (Paul Krugman, et al.) prefer to exit the crisis not by austerity but by more stimulus spending funded by higher deficits. The resulting economic growth, they believe, will automatically lower government budgetary imbalance. The government can then later, if and when needed, impose tax increases and reduced government spending to further offset imbalances. In a growing economy, austerity policies avoid the devastating effects they have in depressed economies (as shown in the recent histories of Greece, Portugal, the United Kingdom, and others).

Setting aside the question of the validity of their argument, what the Keynesians miss is the different purpose of austerity policies. Those policies may not primarily be seeking to overcome crisis or achieve government budgetary balance or resume economic growth. Rather, austerity may be aimed, as argued above, chiefly to (1) shift the burden of paying for crisis and bailouts onto the total population, (2) reduce the economic footprint of the government, and (3) reduce creditors' concerns about rising US debt levels. If austerity policies achieve these objectives, their failure to exit the crisis quickly is a price that corporations and the rich seem more than happy to pay (or, better, have others pay).

Capitalism in Question

The depth and length of the global crisis (now in its sixth year) undermined previous confident assurances and predictions that another deep depression was no longer likely or even possible for modern capitalism. The inherent instability of capitalism overwhelmed and thus again proved the futility of efforts to prevent its crises. The failures of both conventional and extraordinary monetary and fiscal policies to bring Europe, Japan, and the United States out of the crisis challenged glib notions that capitalism's highest authorities have the system "under control." Central banks, international agencies, and national executives charged with economic responsibilities have, since 2007, spoken with assurance and met often, posed for media photos, puffed and threatened, made a few last-minute, stop-gap agreements, resolved to meet again and do more at the next meeting. However, the crisis continued for most people. In many places it has gotten much worse.

Implicitly, at first, millions of people began to question whether capitalism does still "deliver the goods" as its defenders have so long insisted. In the United States, declining job security and benefits for parents coupled with rising education debts and declining job prospects for their children suggest rather a capitalism that "delivers the bads." Widening inequalities of wealth and income that contributed to the crisis have in turn been further aggravated by it. The old ideological mechanisms that for decades had persuaded US citizens that economic hardships were the consequences of their individual decisions and personal failures no longer satisfied growing numbers of people.

The notion that today's economic problems are systemic, that capitalism itself is the problem, returned into the public consciousness and into public debate in ways that had not happened in the United States since the end of World War II.

On the right, in the United States and beyond, the questioning of capitalism has not yet found many strong voices. Instead, right-wing resentments about wealth and income inequality, crises, bailouts for banks, etc., have so far been largely deflected onto increasingly implacable and violent oppositions to government, immigration, the poor, etc. These classic moves of right-wing ideology mobilize a broad coalition of traditional conservatives, nationalists, racists, religious fundamentalists, gun enthusiasts, and so on—the so-called "Tea Party." In the United States, this coalition allies with major capitalist interests in demonizing the government as the evil to be overcome. The alliance provides mass support for the austerity policies that private capitalists prefer for the reasons noted above. It also explains how and why austerity also gets the support even of some who are victimized by that austerity. Attacking the demon government, especially when it's embodied by a black, Democratic president, is the basic Tea Party mantra.

In stark contrast, questioning capitalism was how portions of the left began to find access, slowly and hesitantly, back into mainstream conversation in the United States. They developed new ways of asking questions and focusing criticism. They largely avoided the language, concepts, and imagery associated with earlier forms of anti-capitalism such as those associated with traditional socialism, the USSR, China, and the marginalized, often sectarian groups who remain identified with that tradition. Various sorts of anarchism and unorthodox Marxisms resurfaced and developed followings on the left. They all sympathized with and found ways to formulate critiques of the crisis that focused on its roots in capitalism. Capitalism was a system, they stressed, that one could and should question.

The transition from an implicit to an explicit and widely disseminated systemic criticism of capitalism by the left was an important achievement of the Occupy Wall Street (OWS) movement that emerged in the autumn of 2011. Slogans about the 99 percent confronting the 1 percent condensed a cacophony of very diverse critical attitudes toward the crisis, public policy, and the direction of US economics and politics. A powerful unifying theme arose. The causes of the crisis—unjust bailouts, economic decline, and matching political dysfunction—were also the central problems of our time. Extremely unequal distributions of wealth, income, and power were capitalism's systemic products and likewise explained its problems, crises, and repeated failures to solve them. To get beyond capitalism's instability, inequality, and injustice, system change was necessary.

In Europe, the same global capitalist crisis evolved differently. Inside the United States, overt mass opposition to the crisis, government policy, or capitalism *qua* system was rare; when it occurred, it flared up in short-lived explosions such as the Wisconsin public employee union actions against the governor and in OWS-related activities. By contrast, in Europe mass opposition became nearly continuous after mid-2010 as austerity policies were imposed and various combinations of labor unions, left political parties, and new and often independent social movements went into the streets. Europe has since experienced protests, strikes, mass demonstrations, and general strikes coordinated nationally and sometimes continentally. These mass citizens' actions have been larger, lasted longer, and been better organized than anything seen for at least half a century. As in the United States, especially since OWS, the theme of anti-capitalism has been a notable and growing dimension of these actions.

Moreover, the explanation of the difference between European and US anti-capitalism and anti-austerity movements teaches some important lessons. In Europe after 1945, business and conservative efforts to destroy the labor unions and anti-capitalist parties and movements were far less successful than their counterparts in the United States. Thus, as the current crisis led to austerity, Europeans opposed to austerity and to capitalism were far less disorganized and far less isolated from one another—and likewise less ideologically disarmed. They could and did mobilize millions for classic, visible street actions to advance their criticisms and demands. They could and did plausibly threaten effective electoral action as well.

In contrast, US history after 1945 displays a relentlessly effective destruction of those organizations whose alliance had forced the New Deal on the Roosevelt government. The Congress of Industrial Organizations (CIO) and the socialist and communist parties had then articulated a powerful opposition to austerity intertwined with serious anti-capitalism. Their opposition to austerity was successful. Very high taxes were imposed on corporations and the rich to pay for a major expansion of social welfare for the masses (Social Security, unemployment compensation, and a huge federal jobs program). The contrast between FDR's expansive response to a collapse of the capitalist economy then and the responses of Bush and Obama now could not be starker. What the labor-left alliance of the 1930s failed to achieve was any change at the micro-level of the capitalist system. Major shareholders and their boards of directors remained in full command and control of capitalist enterprises.

Once World War II ended, business and the rich used every possible weapon to roll back the New Deal. From the secured preserves of corporate positions and wealth, they targeted the social forces (labor, socialists, and communists) that had succeeded in raising their taxes and expanding the powers of a mass-based government. One key strategy was to eradicate the socialist and communist parties as effective social movements; this was achieved in the name of intense, Cold War anti-communism. The other key strategy pursued in tandem by business, government, the rich, and the political right entailed attacks on labor unions. Since the Taft-Hartley Act in 1947, countless laws, regulations, and private campaigns contributed to a nearly continuous half-century decline in unions' membership and social influence. If anything, the current crisis through 2012 has intensified that decline.

Thus, US opposition to austerity and capitalism since 2009 differed from European oppositions. The US left had been systematically disorganized, demonized as traitorous, and fragmented. To survive, those who did not abandon their previous political commitments altogether splintered into single-issue social movements (against racism, sexism, homophobia, environmental degradation, etc.). Many sought refuges in more or less safe social enclaves such as the academy, religious institutions, and the arts. When large demonstrations occurred they focused on single issues, minimized or excluded direct criticisms of capitalism, and marginalized or excluded advocacy of alternative economic systems.

For half a century, the capitalist system in the United States enjoyed a free pass from the kinds of debates and criticisms that other systems in the United States experienced. The educational, medical insurance, transportation, energy, and other systems that made up US society had hardly been damaged by those debates and criticisms. Indeed such debate and criticism are widely believed to be signs of social health, indispensable to the improvement of those systems. In contrast, criticism and debate over capitalism as a system were considered taboo and replaced by celebration and cheerleading. Protection from criticism and debate enabled capitalism to indulge its darkest tendencies (deepening inequality, speculation, cronyism, corruption, etc.). Any component system within any society rots when kept immune from criticism and debate.

The economic crisis of capitalism since 2007 has exposed that rot: the immense weaknesses and flaws that had accumulated over the previous half-century. Financial and other mega-corporations rushed to mobilize massive government assistance to save themselves from collapse. Clear to all, that rush mocked the previous era's glib contrast of the private sector as efficient and the public sector as useless or worse. No political gridlock prevented the government from swiftly and nearly unanimously providing those mega-corporations with trillions in loans, guarantees, investments, and other forms of stimulus spending. Yet that same government could not end high and persistent unemployment (for example, by a federal jobs program), or save millions from foreclosure (for example, by managing a transition from ownership to rental for those who needed that), or stop real wages, job benefits, and job security from continuous decline (for example, by regulations freezing them at 2007 levels for the duration of the crisis). These and many other possible solutions—interventions in free-enterprise capitalism—were not considered, let alone examined and debated. The culture of capitalist dominance and the taboo on criticism of capitalism worked to ignore such solutions, let alone the question of economic system change.

The same culture produced a left that is chronically disorganized (a condition often repackaged as anti-authoritarianism to disguise its impotence). It also produced a long left hibernation of the left in a few safe social sites (e.g., academia). These afflictions rendered the left ill-equipped to recognize, let alone mobilize or lead, the US population's increasing alienation from its economic and political leaders and institutions.

However, that alienation did not lead only into widespread self-blame and interpersonal abuse and violence (both epidemics in the United States). While it lacked organizational outlets, growing alienation from capitalism did stimulate mass changes in understanding, consciousness, and feeling. Anti-capitalist impulses and arguments expanded from the few marginalized locales where they had at least partially survived the Cold War. They became increasingly acceptable in public discussions that had formerly ridiculed and dismissed them when not simply excluding them as contemptible mixtures of ignorance and evil. Occupy Wall Street reflected and very significantly magnified that growing acceptance.

Yet another spreading realization provoked by the crisis put capitalism into question. Beyond the crisis (capitalist cycles mean that downturns eventually produce upturns), a suspicion of long-term decline hovers in the basic economic statistics as well as in mass sensibility. The suspicion concerns capital's mobility. After all, western Europe and the United States comprise zones where market conditions plus many decades of workers' struggles eventually yielded high wages. Capital is now relocating to zones in Asia, Latin America, and elsewhere to profit from much lower wage levels. Describing the United States and western Europe as "mature" economies reveals the contrast between their slowing growth and the rising growth in Asia, Latin America, etc. That contrast further reorients capital and production; it relocates growing markets and economic wellbeing abroad.

Many Americans know quite well how cities like Detroit, Cleveland, Camden (New Jersey), and countless others were plunged into decades of economic decline and social collapse in the wake of capital outflows to areas of greater profit. To how many other regions of the United States might similar long-term deterioration be coming? Rising profits for those who benefit from capital mobility versus falling incomes for those hurt by it are basic contributors to the ever-widening inequalities of wealth and income in the United States and western Europe. Both regions face deepening domestic tensions and conflicts as departing capital undermines public and private resources.

Capitalism often rewards enterprises that maximize profit, growth, and/or market share and often punishes those that do not. Capitalism also mostly enables private capitalist enterprises to keep the profits from capital mobility while evading its costs. General Motors, Ford, Chrysler, their suppliers, and their investors were not charged to cover the costs of offsetting the damages to Detroit and its people that resulted from capital outflow. Those costs were socialized, dumped on the US public sector, and, when taxpayers resisted covering those costs of capital mobility, the affected cities were devastated. Capital mobility often delivers shock and awe; it terrorizes whole populations.

As citizens confront the enduring crisis since 2007, they increasingly wonder about whether its depth and duration indicate problems deeper than business cycles. The capital mobility central to capitalism as a system is one such deeper problem.

As citizens wonder about controlling or limiting capital mobility as a national and social danger, they confront again the question of the economic system itself. When rising capitalisms in Europe and the United States drew capital from around the world to fuel their growth, bitter clashes often arose between workers and capitalists over who would benefit, and how much, from that growth. We are likely to have more bitter clashes when the struggle concerns the beneficiaries and losers from economic decline. In any case, the threat and risks of capitalist-driven decline in western Europe and the United States puts the system into question in ways not seen for many decades.

Alternatives to Capitalism

The worsening social pains of austerity together with the increased questioning of capitalism have led to renewed interest in possible alternatives. Sales of Marx's writings have soared. Renewed interest in socialism and socialist parties is widely in evidence. Anarchist rejections of capitalism are in vogue. Public opinion polls show remarkable antipathy for "capitalism" and equally remarkable positive attitudes toward "socialism."

Discontent with the social status quo fuels and largely defines all these expressions. Typically, after some time spent feeling and showing opposition to the status quo, inquiring minds demand some concrete, feasible alternatives to capitalism. They wish at least to complement their opposition to capitalism with some positive affirmation of a better system. Critiques of capitalism, its crisis, and the inadequacy of "solutions" such as bailouts and austerity have matured significantly across the last five years. They now include explorations and advocacy of transition from capitalism toward such alternatives.

However, traditional socialism and communism, as exemplified in the USSR, eastern Europe, and the People's Republic of China, are not widely accepted as desirable alternatives. This reflects partly their actual histories and partly their demonization by the last 70 years of hegemonic anti-communism across most of the world. The classical dichotomy pitting private property and markets (defined as capitalism) against national property and central planning (defined as socialism or communism) seems increasingly secondary to critics of capitalism today. Those critics sense that government ownership of productive property and central planning may be neither necessary nor sufficient to secure the socialist alternative to private capitalism they had hoped for. They are also influenced by recent critiques of classical socialism from the left (see, for example, Stephen Resnick and Richard Wolff, *Class Theory and History: Capitalism and Communism in the USSR*, New York and London: Routledge Publishers, 2002). Such criticism explains how and why state ownership and planning can be exploitative and oppressive, presenting a state capitalism masked as a socialist alternative to capitalism.

In other words, something other than the ownership of means of production must change (from private to state) and something other than the distribution mechanism must change (from market exchange to planning) if transition to another, basically different economic system is to occur. Something else, perhaps yet more basic, must change to redirect the economic, political, and cultural behaviors of both enterprises and governments onto different tracks yielding systematically non-capitalist institutions and individuals.

The demands for concrete alternatives to capitalism and the critiques of classical socialism and communism from the left have renewed interest in and developed new conceptions of *cooperative* enterprises. The idea is simple. Basic enterprise decisions are no longer to be monopolized by the major shareholders and the boards of directors those shareholders select, the norm in capitalist corporations. Instead, they are to be democratized. Workers are to become, collectively, their own board of directors in fully cooperative enterprises. As such, they would democratically decide what to produce, and how and where, and they would distribute the surpluses (or profits) generated in and by their enterprise.

Such workers' self-directed enterprises (WSDEs) already have a well-developed website, *democracyatwork.info*. It shows past and present examples of functioning WSDEs and examines how they are formed, the problems they encounter, the solutions they have tested, and so on. The website provides a continuously expanding bibliography, research papers on WSDEs, frequently asked questions about WSDEs and responses to them, links to the many organizations of cooperative and collective enterprises that now engage many millions, and much more.

WSDEs represent the goal of a transition beyond capitalism at the micro-level, inside the enterprises that produce the goods and services upon which modern civilization depends. In such a transition, workers are activated continuously. They must change the structure of decision-making inside the enterprise and then sustain the new structure. Workers in WSDEs retain ongoing responsibility for the enterprise's successful functioning. To that end, they must overcome the complex social resistances to establishing and sustaining democratic workplaces. These resistances include far more than the private ownership of means of production and various market mechanisms. They include the many features of the economy, politics, and culture that, over many years, adjusted to become supportive of the capitalist structure of enterprises. In politics, the executive, administrative, and judicial branches of government at local, regional, national, and international levels need major changes to instead become supportive of WSDEs. The same applies to cultural institutions such as schools, mass media, and so on.

For example, consider school systems whose elite institutions have long been geared to educate future top executive layers of capitalist corporations. Those institutions teach the skills and habits of enterprise overview, direction, design, and management. School systems would have to reorient and redesign curricula and differently prepare teachers if their social role were to equip *all* workers to perform the directorial functions assigned to *all* within WSDEs. To take another example, laws governing the ownership of enterprises (whether ownership be private or public, centralized or decentralized, individual or collective) will need to be changed so that all ownership must respect the rule that all productive workers are also—and exclusively—members of an enterprise's board of directors.

WSDEs organize economic decisions to serve the interests of the people by eliminating the decision-making roles and positions of capitalists understood as the shareholders and their representatives, the boards of directors of capitalist corporations. The people themselves—in the persons of enterprise workers and residents of communities interdependent with the enterprise—become the only direct decision makers. Inside the enterprise, the workers become their own board of directors who receive and distribute the surpluses (profits) generated by the enterprise. This represents the end of exploitation defined as follows: any enterprise organization in which the producers of surpluses/profits are different people from those who obtain and distribute such surpluses/profits.

The set of decisions to be made by self-directing workers also includes determining what the enterprise will produce, which technology it will use, where production will occur, and who will receive what portions of the distributed surplus. All workers in an enterprise will democratically participate in reaching those decisions. In addition, because those decisions impact communities and residences in various areas of the enterprise's activity, the democratic governing institutions in those communities must also participate in reaching enterprise decisions. Likewise, because governing institutions in communities make decisions impacting enterprises, the boards of the enterprises must also participate in reaching community governance decisions. The entire structure and operation of economic and political decision-making will need to be reconstituted—the very meaning of "democratic decision-making" redeveloped—to realize an economic system based on WSDEs.

Workers—as members of enterprises and/or members of residential communities—will finally command the basic decision-making positions in a post-capitalist system based on

WSDEs. As individual workers, they will dispose of their wage and salary incomes. Likewise, as members of the enterprise's board of directors, they will dispose of its surplus or profits. Since the state's revenues and hence its ability to function depend chiefly on taxes drawn from wages, salaries, and enterprise surpluses/profits, the state finally becomes dependent on and thus ultimately accountable to the people. That was always the democratic dream and goal. Capitalism blocked the realization of democracy in large part because it made the state and some political parties particularly dependent upon and accountable chiefly to a small minority: capitalists and those (top executives and major shareholders) made rich by capitalists' distributions of surplus to them. By means of a transition from capitalism to WSDEs, economic democracy partners with and thereby realizes political democracy.

Political democracy has been repeatedly limited, constrained, and corrupted by capitalism. That happened because political democracy based on universal suffrage *could* redistribute or reclaim politically the profits concentrated in capitalists' hands by the economy. The masses by their votes *could* negate capitalism. To prevent that, capitalists had to control politics. They utilized their financial and related resources to buy politicians, parties, mass media, lobbyists, think tanks, public relations experts, etc. Thus, democracy with capitalism remained mostly formal, a veneer to mask the absence of real democracy. To move from formal to real, political democracy must be intertwined with economic democracy inside enterprises.

WSDEs would also likely make decisions that would render the economic and political landscapes of modern societies quite different from what they now display. For example, a major influence on the personal distribution of income and wealth in those societies is the distribution of the surplus generated by enterprises. Boards of directors and major shareholders now determine what portions of that surplus are paid out as dividends and interest to stockholders and bondholders. They likewise determine the pay packages and bonuses given to top executives. In WSDEs, it is extremely unlikely that worker-directors would pay huge sums to a few top executives while most workers have difficulties covering basic family expenses. Likewise, they would have different attitudes toward dividend and interest payments out of surpluses. In short, personal income distributions would likely change significantly toward greater equality.

WSDEs would also be likely to evaluate alternative technologies and product mixes rather differently from how that is done in capitalist corporations today. Major shareholders and boards of directors are often located far from the sites of an enterprise's actual production and often able to insulate themselves and their families from toxicities associated with alternative technologies and alternative final products. They are thus more likely to choose a technology or a product for production that boosts the firm's bottom line even if it has toxic effects, whereas the worker-directors in a WSDE would be less likely to do so since they would less easily be able to evade those effects.

Major shareholders and their boards of directors have traditionally valued profits over any dimension of the work process and its impact on workers. Worker-directors in WSDEs, being as personally influenced by the process of work as by its profits, would evaluate the totality of the enterprise rather differently. They would make countless enterprise decisions differently and thereby generate altogether different lives for themselves, their families, and their communities.

Thus WSDEs represent an attractive micro-level alternative to a crisis-cum-austerity-ridden and declining capitalism. With or without the classic macro-alternatives of socialized productive property and economic planning, WSDEs offer a positive complement to the critiques of austerity programs and capitalism as a system that have emerged since 2009, when this book's first edition was published. Capitalism hit the fan in this crisis, and the consequences for social change keep mounting.

INTRODUCTION (2009)

The world is now suffering the second major crisis of capitalism in 75 years (not to mention the dozen smaller economic downturns in the US alone between the Great Depression of the 1930s and today). The crash that began in 2008 has exploded many beliefs carefully cultivated by academics and massively publicized by business and political leaders via the media subservient to them. The idea that modern capitalism was no longer subject to crashes with devastating social costs is gone. This latest boom gone bust dissolved the myth of a new kind of economy in the US and the UK bringing the world ever-growing wealth by spreading its institutions of private property, multinational corporations, and market freedoms. The notion that government deregulation would free the economy to grow has turned into the desperate hope that massive new government re-regulations and government economic interventions can save capitalism in the US, UK, and beyond from utter collapse.

In short order, the country's largest insurance company, largest banks, and largest automobile company went bankrupt, in fact if not also legally in each case. Their collapses—and those of many other US corporations—exposed the massive leadership failures of their boards of directors. The US government placed the biggest (the infamous "too big to fail" crew) on life support with massive infusions of taxpayers' money. Obama keeps promising to return them soon—once public money and concessions wrung from workers "restore their profitability"—back to the control of the same private corporate boards of directors who delivered them into bankruptcy.

Not all economists and others who paid attention to changes in the US economy over recent decades joined in that blindly uncritical celebration of all things capitalistic called "mainstream economic analysis." But until the crisis erupted, economic activity plummeted, and millions lost jobs and homes, the critics had few platforms, few opportunities, and thus only marginal influence. However, the magazine *Monthly Review*, begun with Albert

Einstein's help in 1949 and published regularly ever since, kept its critical edge. In 2005 it opened a website to add an electronic magazine to its publications. Shortly thereafter, I began to publish short, topically focused articles there.

They critically analyzed the US political economy that I believed was in deepening danger of collapse. I have published critiques of the US political economy regularly since then. Most of them are collected in this volume. Gradually, after 2005, my writing goals changed. As the crisis loomed, I shifted away from exposing the economic problems and weaknesses that the mainstream celebrants of capitalism always missed or denied. I began to examine the depth, implications, and costs of the crisis to counter the mainstream insistences that the crisis would be averted, then that it would be short and shallow, then that the "bottom" had been reached, and so on. Finally, when the immensity of the crisis could no longer be hidden or ignored, even by the mainstream, my focus turned to criticism of the solutions proposed by first the Bush and then Obama administrations. Most recently, I have highlighted those solutions *not* attempted by both administrations. My point is to show why they deserve the discussion, debate, and application that the mainstream avoids in the US, UK, and beyond.

This book offers readers two different services, according to how you read it. The article titles listed in the Contents invite readers to pursue those aspects of this great crisis that interest them most. Teachers seeking to provide students with short, condensed, and readily accessible treatments of those aspects may find many of these articles suitable. At the same time, within each topical section of the book, the individual articles appear in the chronological order of their publication. Reading them in that order allows readers to follow the buildup to crisis, the crash itself, and then the political economy of crisis responses as viewed by a critic of the system. It's a bit like reading a critic's diary of the crisis.

Today, the mainstream of academic, business, political, and media leaders mostly celebrates how government programs are "solving" the crisis just as before it had celebrated capitalism as never needing government "intrusion." Democrats have replaced Republicans in Washington; Keynesians have replaced traditional laissez-faire champions; the pendulum that swung rightward after the 1970s is now swinging back to the center. An unreconstructed fundamentalist minority fights the mainstream shift by insisting on the old religion of "private enterprise and free markets" as if the crisis were a minor blip or maybe even the fault of the demon government.

However, the crisis has so shaken most people that discussion about the economy can no longer be entirely contained and monopolized by the mainstream and the fundamentalists. The issues raised by the crisis go far beyond the stale old debates between those favoring more versus less government. The capitalist system itself has been placed in question. Conservatives inadvertently contributed to this questioning by pasting the label "socialist" on Obama to reactivate their demoralized base. More importantly, many on the political center-left and left rediscovered the importance and relevance of examining different kinds of socialism as systemic alternatives to a crisis-prone capitalism.

We critics now have an exceptional opportunity. We can develop further an already sizeable audience produced by capitalist crisis. That will depend in large part on our ability to show clearly that the crisis is systemic and that systemic change is among the "solutions" that should be considered. Books like this aim to make sure that public debate in and over this economic crisis will not be constricted to the narrow contest between more and less government. After all, what hit the fan was global capitalism, a system designed and managed by private enterprises and government working closely together. This book's goal is to offer new and compelling arguments for thinking that systemic problems require systemic solutions. The articles elaborate and supplement the core themes of *Capitalism Hits the Fan*, a documentary film that I made in 2009 with the Media Education Foundation (www.mediaed.org). The articles also reflect a large body of research (www.rdwolff.com).

PART I: ROOTS OF A SYSTEM'S CRISIS

Today's global capitalist crisis has many, deep roots in the cultural, political, and economic processes that interact to comprise our world. The essays included in Part I highlight the complexities and the depth of those roots. The crisis is systemic in that it is a structural and recurring feature of capitalism. It is also systemic in its emergence from basic contours of the history of the United States. Yet it is particularly rooted in a crucial shift that happened in the capitalist system during the 1970s when the average real wages of US workers permanently stopped their century of steady increases.

The end of rising wages had staggering consequences as it interacted with the institutions, attitudes, and behaviors of the larger US society and the rest of the world. Those consequences were all the more socially destructive because they were not generally recognized or understood as connected to the sea change in wages. No genuinely public debate about that change—and the social costs of allowing it—has occurred to date. Instead, the politicians, major media, and academic mainstreams repeated celebrations of capitalism's efficient markets.

The social problem of a society suddenly ending a century of rising real wages was thus responded to individually by households, businesses, and governments. They responded with no consciousness of that social problem and its consequences. How they did so, as illustrated in Part I's essays, culminated in today's crisis. Individual responses are not only inadequate to solve social problems. They often worsen those problems until much costlier social solutions can no longer be avoided. So it has been in the US and beyond with capitalism's latest crisis.

One goal of the essays gathered here is to provoke and inform a social debate about the causes of the crisis, one that does not shy away from questioning its systemic nature.

The Political Pendulum Swings,
the Alienation Deepens

11 May 2005

F DR's New Deal changed the tone and shape of US politics into a kind of moderate social democracy. Desperate to end the Great Depression nightmare, US voters secured FDR and the Democrats in power. The right wing, in and out of the Republican Party, dove into decline, agonized for years, slowly regrouped, and then revived. With Reagan and then Bush, it could finally redefine the tone and shape of US politics—this time to reverse FDR's legacy. Today, liberals in and out of the Democratic Party hope to retrace a parallel path to reverse Reagan–Bush. The pendulum of US politics swings while its foundation remains unchanged, thereby alienating citizens from politics ever more deeply.

As FDR rose to dominance, the political pendulum swung left. The right wing recoiled from public life. A period of severe self-doubt broadened into a hopelessness that its political aims would ever again become the top policy goals for the nation. Only after a dozen years of bewildered political limbo would the Cold War and hysterical anti-communism provide right-wingers with a slow way back to power. They could then begin to undermine and displace the deep national consciousness that the 1930s depression was a social disaster for which private enterprise was to blame and state intervention the solution. The right wing's mantra was to play a different blame game: denounce the left for supporting and the liberals for failing to foresee and protect against the "threats" to national security entailed by China's "fall to the communists," the Soviet acquisition of nuclear weapons and then space technology, and so on. The revived post-war US economy plus hyped anti-communism offered new possibilities and new resources for right-wing resurgence. At first, businesses heavily funded think tanks to attack and undermine the popular, journalistic, and academic mentalities inherited from New Deal dominance. Then, they branched out to fund efforts to build mass organizations of the right based on global militarism, fundamentalist religion, and reinvigorated racism. The latter evolved into movements using new technologies (such as direct mail) to tap mass funding that could supplement business money. The political pendulum began to move rightward.

To perfect its mechanisms, organizations, and finances, the right needed continually to adjust the demonizations of its enemies (from the John Birch Society's anti-left witch hunts to Reagan targeting the "evil empire"). When anti-communism lost its usefulness after the collapse of Eastern Europe in the late 1980s, effective demonization politics required a new target. This time, patriotism, fundamentalist religion, racism, and militarism—supplemented by anti-gay and then, after 2001, anti-terrorism hysterias—coalesced against "the liberals" directly and explicitly. Before, the right's attack on communism had only indirectly targeted "liberals" as sympathizers/fellow travelers/dupes of communism and socialism (treated as synonyms). With Bush, the right could more openly proclaim its primary domestic agenda: to reverse the New Deal in a fundamental reactionary switch. What anti-communism had only partially achieved, anti-liberalism should complete.

Culminating in the current Bush regime, the right-wing ascendancy plunged the New Deal coalition and its descendants into the same position the right had found itself in by the mid-1930s. The 1980s were years of the liberals' deepening despondency, self-doubt, and political hopelessness. The Clinton years only briefly masked the desperation of their situation. The right had what seemed to be an unbeatable strategic game plan: an economy redirected to profits and the rich (who provided campaign funds) coupled with fundamentalist religion (that provided solace, meaning, uplift, and hope to the masses ever more stressed by Bush's economic and social policies).

The more Bush policies benefited business, profits, and the rich, the more those policies cost workers: reduced real wages,

deepened debt, extended working hours, strained family relationships, and reduced prospects for their and their children's
futures. Yet, at the same time, Bush's carefully structured public
relations successfully positioned him as the champion of the
fundamentalist religion toward which stressed workers were
turning in numbers sufficient to give Bush electoral victories.
Indeed, liberals were effectively pilloried as disrespectful of religion and thus, by extension, of working people and their
problems. The Democrats were exposed as offering no real solutions, no real alternatives to what the Republican right was
already doing. There was little excitement among non-funda-
mentalists to vote for Democrats (seen quite rightly as only
slightly less harsh Republicans), while there was intense feeling
among fundamentalists to vote for Bush as their churches' best
representative and supporter. The Democrats deteriorated into
the kind of spineless me-too party that the Republicans had
been under Roosevelt.

Just as the post-New Deal right had to wait for the Cold
War to offer a way forward, the post-Reagan liberals had to wait
for Bush's exploitation of 9/11 to unravel. And indeed, when it
did, the political pendulum began a leftward shift. Bush
displaced blame for not having prevented 9/11 by positioning
himself instead as the nation's guardian aggressively "taking the
fight to our terrorist enemies." The invasion of Iraq however
failed its purposes by producing foreign opposition, international isolation, and growing US losses. Eventually, Cindy
Sheehan put Bush on the defensive. As Bush moved to use 9/11
domestically to speed up his regime's reversal of the New Deal,
mass support for Social Security also put him on the defensive.
Lastly, the spectacular exposé of federal government incompetence (or worse) in New Orleans put Bush on the defensive yet
again. He had failed as guardian of the people's security, failed
to prevent grotesque incompetence and cronyism from corrupt-
ing his administration, and looked like God might NOT be on
his side. Not only did Katrina hand the Democrats an arsenal
of anti-Bush weaponry, it also revealed (deepening) racial and

income divisions. When government officials fail to hide or effectively minimize popular awareness of such divisions, they anger the more comfortable voters who (consciously or unconsciously) expect insulation from the disturbing reality in return for their political support. Such voters become vulnerable to Democratic blandishments—how Democrats will "bring together" (that is, hide again)—what Republicans have revealed as (and thereby get blamed for) a divided society.

So now the Democrats may acquire the minimal courage to keep the pendulum swinging their way by gathering up the strands of Bush failures into a successful electoral presentation of themselves as the necessary antidote and corrective. In this, they seek to replicate exactly what the Republicans accomplished in the decades after 1935. After all, to win in the US electoral system usually requires only a few percentage points of voters to switch parties.

The old and tired oscillations between "liberals" and "conservatives," between Democrats and Republicans, remain the basis of mainstream US politics. Pendulum swings work now for Republicans, now for Democrats. What the swings leave unchallenged and unchanged is the class structure of the country—the capitalist arrangements of production that divide people and products into workers versus capitalists and wages versus profits. No significant political force connects this capitalist system of production to social problems. No such force advocates changing the class structure as part of a solution to those problems.

When class structures neither change nor even seem open to change, the endless political oscillations eventually convey their superficiality to the public. Politics then loses all contact with basic questions of choosing among alternative social structures and among alternative goals and strategies for social change. At best, politics interests specific sub-groups only if, when, and so long as some specific issue of immediate personal concern is at stake (abortion, gun control, gay marriage, oil prices, etc.). At worst—and the worst is what we increasingly

experience—politics pits irrelevant tweedledums against twee-
dledees, cynically advertised candidate #1 vs public-relations-
driven #2. People then turn away first from political activism,
then from participation and information, and finally even from
the passivity of mere voting. A mass alienation from politics altogether deepens, immune to the vapid exhortations to civic duty.
Politics descends into a special branch of business where politicians make money and advance careers by mutually profitable
relations with other businesses. This alienation—and the cari-
cature politics it both reflects and enables—will remain unless
and until a class-based politics emerges to contest for power.

Dividing the Conservative Coalition

5 August 2005

The Bush government, itself a coalition of the willing, cobbles together four different streams of conservatives. Like all coalitions, it is vulnerable to events. Patrick Buchanan, the journal *National Interest,* and the think tank Cato Institute, are conservatives against Bush's Iraq policy. Similarly, the conservative American Enterprise Institute and the Heritage Foundation criticize Bush's fiscal policies. Moderate Republicans oppose the party's extreme right wing on social policies and state-church relations. Strained also by other divisions, the coalition is vulnerable to divide-and-conquer interventions if its opponents clearly understand the different origins and goals of each coalition "partner."

The first conservative stream is chiefly economic. It comprises that part of the US business community (plus its media and academic hangers-on) that seeks to roll back FDR's New Deal. These interests distrust and attack state economic interventions that are not subordinated to private business needs and dictates. They favor deregulation of industry, reduction of worker protections (e.g., pensions, health and safety rules, etc.), cutting taxes on business profits and dividends, raising tax deductions for investments, and so on. From Taft-Hartley in 1947 through the current attack on Social Security, these "conservatives" relentlessly undo the "welfare state."

The second stream—"neo-conservatives"—is different. For Richard Perle, "conserving" the US requires reshaping the entire world in its image:

> We are going to have to take the war against [the terrorists] often to other people's territory, and all of the norms of international order make it difficult to do that. So the president has to reshape fundamental attitudes toward those norms, or we are going to have our hands tied by an antiquated institution [the traditional international system] that is not capable of defending us (*Christian Science Monitor* website).

Such global entitlement flows from a belief in the US's absolute social, economic, and military superiority. Not only *should* the US realize its global ambitions, but its sole super-power status makes that possible. The first chance, in 1945, was lost in a failure of nerve (FDR's and Truman's); the second chance after the USSR's collapse was also missed (Clinton's fault). The last and best chance to make up for lost opportunities is now.

The third conservative stream emerged in reaction to the 1960s when young people weakened the traditional subordination of women and black Americans, sexual taboos, institutionalized religions, and the authoritarianism of schools and the government. "Social" conservatives mounted sustained campaigns *against* abortion, affirmative action, and non-traditional sexual relationships and *for* the renewal of traditional families, traditional religiosity, and traditional schooling. According to Rev. Bob Enyart, pastor of Denver Bible Church, "Christians who carefully study the Bible are best qualified to teach the world how it should be governed."

The fourth stream arose in the 1980s and 1990s as a backlash against multiculturalism. New mass immigrations—from Asia, eastern Europe, and central America (especially Mexico)—demanded some accommodation of their different modes of thought, speech, and cultural norms; multiculturalism was one response. A new wave of conservatives countered by insisting on the absolute superiority of received US practices (English exclusivity, only "classic" school curricula, and so on). They revived earlier but still active nativist and isolationist traditions. In polarized debates, multiculturalists' appeals for toleration of difference sometimes expanded to assertions of the relativity not only of cultural values but of science, knowledge, and truth itself. Multiculturalists thus sometimes embraced postmodernism. Outraged conservatives reacted by reaffirming the absolute superiority of US (or "Western") culture and what it has established as truth. For the religious fundamentalists among them, that meant a return to biblical revelation. For the more secular, it meant a return to the scientific method and the objective truth it had established and upon which US society was built. By contrast, multiculturalism (and postmodernism, too) was condemned for leading civilization backward into "pre-modern" superstition and obscurantism. For the Ayn Rand Institute, multiculturalism seeks to obliterate the value of a free, industrialized civilization (which today exists in the West and elsewhere), by declaring that such a civilization is no better than primitive tribalism. More deeply, it seeks to incapacitate a mind's ability to distinguish good from evil, to distinguish that which is life-promoting from that which is life-negating.

Over the last 25 years, these four streams formed a hegemonic coalition within US society. Neither Bush nor the revived Republican Party accomplished this coalition; rather it produced them. Chief among the social changes that enabled conservative hegemony were (1) declining average wages since the mid-1970s and (2) consequently greater inequality of wealth and income. With their living standards and relative social positions thus threatened, most American families sent more household members out to work. Women took first jobs or left part-time for full-time employment, men and women took second and third jobs, and everyone worked more hours. When that did not suffice, American families borrowed beyond anything ever seen anywhere. The resulting exhaustion, interpersonal tensions, and financial anxieties yielded crises of divorce, alienation, depression, drug dependence, and abuse.

Desperate Americans welcomed politicians delivering tax cuts (however modest) and heroic wars "to save us" from evil. Many turned to religious leaders promising salvation or at least solace. Fundamentalist churches refashioned their image as "loving communities" beckoning Americans who had ever greater difficulty finding community or love anywhere else. New audiences cheered celebrations of "traditional values" that sounded increasingly like battle cries for a return to the good old days before workers had unmanageable stress and debt. Of course, other factors also facilitated conservative hegemony.

The collapse of the USSR, 9/11, and the business concentration of US mass media all fostered or reinforced the coalition. Conservative hegemony also depended on successfully dividing the coalition that was the Democratic Party and thereby removing it as an effective opposition.

Yet divisions and tensions also beset the conservative coalition. While some fundamentalist religious leaders share the neocons' enthusiasm for US global "dominion," they don't all agree on what dominion means. Not all advocates of rolling back the New Deal see benefits from denouncing multiculturalism. Not a few Christian fundamentalists find their alliance with opponents of Social Security and with neocons uncomfortable or worse.

The strategy of the coalition's opponents can include aggravating its divisions and tensions. Oppositional think tanks might devise arguments against anti-New Deal business interests that document their support for the social agenda of religious fundamentalists. Oppositional media might weaken the appeal of anti-multiculturalist movements by stressing their alliance with neocon imperialists and their costly war policies. Systematically exposing religious fundamentalism as a key support for the anti-New Deal assault on such programs as Social Security might well yield powerful slogans for politicians seeking to divide and weaken the conservative coalition. Connecting neocon wars with rising federal power, taxes, deficits, and falling social support programs such as student loans and public services might well do likewise.

Of course, a positive alternative program and a counterhegemonic coalition are the crucial requirements to defeat the conservative coalition. Yet, divisive intervention—based on a clear grasp of the coalition's fragility—can make a difference. A successful strategy to reverse the current direction of social change requires both positive and negative components.

Economic Inequality and US Politics

13 December 2005

O ver the last 25 years, economic inequality in the US grew. As the gap between haves and have-nots worsened, social injustices and tensions increased. As usual, politicians in power have devised projects and campaigns designed to distract attention from these realities. Opposition politicians wonder whether they dare attack growing inequality and champion programs for *less* economic inequality. But before we do the politics, let's do the numbers.

The data on Americans' income inequality are stark. According to the US Census Bureau, comparing data for 1967 and 2001, the share of total income flowing to the bottom 60 percent of US households fell from 32 to 27 percent. The share of total income flowing to the top 5 percent rose from under 18 to over 22 percent. The share of income to the "middle" barely changed. In short, the high-income receivers got big raises, while the majority low-income earners got even less than before. The middle struggled not to follow the poor downward even as it watched the rich rise ever further out of reach.

Wealth in the US—what Americans own rather than what they earn—is even more unequally distributed than income. Thus, in 2001, the top 5 percent of Americans owned 57.7 percent of the total wealth (assets minus liabilities). The bottom 50 percent owned a stunning 2.8 percent of the total. Wealth inequality, like income inequality, got significantly worse over the last 25 years.

The growing inequality between the rich, on the one hand, and the middle and poor, on the other, helps to explain many important features of recent US history. Since real hourly wages (money wages adjusted for price changes) fell across most of the last quarter century, working-class families sent more members out to work and also worked more hours. When that was not enough to maintain, let alone improve, living standards, those families took on massive new debts (via credit cards and home loans). Work exhaustion aggravated by debt anxieties worsened the stress levels across US households.

Meanwhile, the richest 10 to 20 percent minority can afford expenditures for "lifestyles" that the majority can barely imagine with a mix of envy and resentment. The Bush regime secures its chief *financial base* by delivering huge rewards to that minority (via tax cuts, deregulation, military spending, subsidies, and so on). The Bush Republicans secure the needed *mass base* by effectively mobilizing the majority's resentment and envy into hostility against the urban, bicoastal rich labeled as "liberals" and Democrats (accused of taxing the middle to subsidize the lazy poor). Thus, Republicans paint Democrats as people who sneer at the struggling working class, denigrate its religious commitments, and ridicule its desperate efforts to reverse the disintegration of its households (read: its support of "family values"). The liberals and Democrats get pictured as anti-religion, elitist, gay-friendly, and sexually licentious. Anti-sexism is attacked as anti-family. Anti-racism is equated with government programs discriminating against the middle-income and poor whites. The anti-Iraq war movement is transformed into disrespect and non-support for working-class soldiers "defending their country."

The economic difficulties besetting the US working class turn many of its members away from politics and even from merely voting. Others respond to the Republicans' claims. In these two ways, enough workers abandon their formerly Democratic party affiliations to enable Republicans to win elections, expand state power, and use it to serve their economic and political bases. Meanwhile, Democratic leaders fear to lose financial support from the rich—their financial base, too, in a system of money-dependent political campaigns. Thus the spectacle of how little they do to blunt, let alone stop, the Republican successes. Democratic leaders refuse to make the workers' deteriorating economic conditions the basis for a campaign to redistribute wealth and income back to them. Democratic politicians thus mostly lose; and, when they win, they do so by aping the Republicans.

Yet, pushing this political game too far risks backfiring. Some signs suggest that this may be happening. Shrinking polls show that Bush's mass base is increasingly reduced to Christian fundamentalists, gun-control opponents, anti-environmentalists, and gung-ho militarists. They are fewer but harsher, more extreme. The problem is that they dislike and are, in turn, scorned by the rich and traditionally conservative backers of the Republican party, its main financial base. The latter wants first and foremost to limit state power. Big business mostly wants to keep the private sector that it dominates unthreatened by a strong state that might fall into the hands of opponents of that domination, leftist or rightist. With no left to fear in the US today, the Republicans' moneyed financial base increasingly distrusts a Bush regime that keeps expanding state power chiefly to secure its own political survival by pandering to its shrinking mass base. As that base draws back, the Bush regime must offer ever shadier deals to ever shadier lobbyists and their clients: exchanging government support for campaign contributions, quid pro quo.

Conservative Republicans are thus backing away from Bush. So far, they are attacking mostly his regime's increasing shady dealings: "Republican power in the service of lobbyists who, in their K Street habitat, are in the service of rent seekers—interests eager to bend public power for their private advantage" (George Will, "On K Street Conservatism," *Newsweek* 17 October 2005: 78). Such conservatives will become increasingly interested in those centrist Democrats who promise to reduce state power. If this continues, the Bush era's days are indeed numbered. Power may then shift to Democrats who will limit the state and protect the private sector's status quo. Those Democrats will get considerable financial backing formerly provided to the Republicans. That—plus the traditional Democratic mass base, i.e., stressed workers looking for any change that might relieve the pressures they face—might then win enough elections to prevail as the next phase of American politics. If so, the Republican mass base will feel rejected and abused once again, thereby providing opportunities for the next generation of right-wing revivalist politicians.

Whatever the benefits of a defeat for Bush Republicanism, the deeper problems will remain. Democrats will not likely dare to jeopardize their return to power by any significant redistribution of wealth and power. If so, they will thereby invite another erosion of their mass base as workers turn their frustration and anger over economic inequality against the Democrats in power. That is, after all, how Reagan and the Bushes came to power. The big question remains: will the mass of Americans continue to tolerate these oscillations as the nature and limits of the nation's politics?

Reform vs. Revolution: Settling Accounts

10 February 2006

US liberals—left, right, and center—have always justified reformism on the grounds that it is realistic. "Nothing more than a limited set of reforms is achievable in the present circumstances" has been their mantra. They insist that efforts toward more basic "revolutionary" social changes would be successfully resisted by the capitalist establishment, would not be supported by the masses, and thus are irresponsibly utopian provocations to right-wing reaction. In contrast, reforms can be won; they can actually make life better. So the reformers have sought to reduce unemployment, raise wages, improve working conditions, reduce racial and gender discrimination, improve educational opportunities, healthcare, housing, and so on. They boast about the reforms they have achieved: further evidence for them that reform was and is realistic and revolution a dangerous delusion.

Thus liberals and even most radicals have kept their struggles over the last century reformist by excluding revolutionary demands to end exploitation in the Marxian sense. That is, they have refused to demand that workers in each and every enterprise take over the receipt and distribution of the surpluses that workers produce, the "value added" by laboring activity, or what corporations prefer to call their "profits." The revolutionary demands—that workers need and deserve to become their own bosses and thereby to eliminate the class differences and antagonisms between capitalists and workers—were dismissed or denounced by reformists. The profits had to be left in the hands of the capitalists: the price, in a sense, to be paid for reforms.

In the wake of the decline of left and labor movements in the US over recent years, reformism strikes many as the very most we can hope for, if even that is possible. For them, revolutionary goals seem even less "realistic" now than before. Yet, on closer examination, the exact opposite case can be made. Ironically, as we shall see, the Bush regime is making it.

Since the Great Depression, reformers in the US have struggled for rising wages and all those government supports that made up the New Deal then and the "welfare state" ever since. While they failed to achieve many reforms, they did achieve enough of them to support their advocacy of reformist politics. Reform, they said, "worked." Their revolutionary critics reacted with two basic points. First, they declared it a strategic tragedy to have limited mass mobilizations to mere reformism when a revolutionary program might well have garnered support and thereby built a revolutionary movement. Their second point was to warn that so long as achieved reforms benefiting workers left intact the underlying capitalist organization of production, the capitalists could and would soon attack and eventually eliminate the reforms.

What the current Bush regime gives the revolutionaries is the proof for their second point. Step by relentless step, and despite occasional failures (such as last year's assault on Social Security), the forces behind Bush have reversed the reforms. More reversals are underway. The social opposition to the program of reversal appears too weak, disorganized, and ineffective to do more than slow its pace.

The rising inequalities of wealth and income in the US especially since 1975, based on the rise of capitalist profits relative to workers' wages, have had two key effects. To maintain, let alone raise, living standards, workers have taken more jobs, worked longer hours, and accumulated enormous debts. The resulting exhaustion and financial anxieties of working families have sapped the energies, resources, and organizations needed to secure the reforms won earlier. At the same time, rising profits have provided capitalists with the additional resources, confidence, and incentives needed to undo most of the reforms won over the last 75 years.

Today it is political "realism" to question reformism. History is settling accounts in the reformism versus revolution debate. Henceforth, social movements seeking reforms will need to include demands for revolutionary changes as necessary means to secure those reforms they can achieve. Otherwise workers will not regain confidence in reformist movements. No longer will it be an abstract proposition to combine reform and revolution within one political strategy for social change. That combination is becoming the only realistic left position.

Exit-Poll Revelations

13 November 2006

Exit polls conducted at last week's elections reveal the contradictions and limits of the Democrats' victories. As reported in the *New York Times* (9 November 2006: P7), the four fifths of US voters who are white preferred Republicans (52 to 48 percent), while blacks, Hispanics, and Asians chose Democrats (by 89 to 11, 70 to 30, and 62 to 38 respectively). Looking at voters' income levels showed that the lower the family income, the larger the Democratic margin. Families earning below $15,000 preferred Democrats over Republicans by 69 to 31 percent. As incomes rose, the Democratic advantage fell: families with incomes over $100,000—23 percent of voters— preferred Republicans over Democrats by 52 to 48 percent. Democrats owe their victories in no small measure to the poorer and the less white among us.

Yet, consider these contradictory numbers for families with very high annual incomes ($150,000–200,000). Those living in the East preferred Democrats by 63 to 37 percent, a remarkable shift from 2004 when they preferred Republicans by 50 to 48 percent. For Eastern families earning over $200,000, the 2006 results showed a preference for Democrats of 50 to 48 percent, compared to 2004 when those families preferred Republicans by 56 to 40. Exit polls in the South, West, and Midwest, while less extreme, showed similar shifts. Many of the richest Americans changed their party preferences over the last two years.

The richest Americans provide most of the contributions funding Congressional campaigns. The Democrats got more votes in no small part because they got more money from those richer households: money used to offset both heavy Republican spending on TV advertising and media "reportage" that favored Republicans.

The exit polls therefore pose an obvious question: why did so many of the richest families switch their contributions and their votes to Democrats? *Slate* magazine's Daniel Gross refers to "angry, well-off, well-educated yuppies, generally clustered on the coasts, who were funneling windfalls from Bush tax cuts into the campaigns of Democrats and preparing to vote for those who would raise taxes on their capital gains, their incomes, and their estates." Gross thinks that hatred of Bush trumped their economic self-interest. If so, the question is why. Here is one possible answer.

What Bush accomplished was rarely a problem for his richest constituents. It was rather the manner, speed, and costs of his accomplishments that provoked growing criticism, distaste, and derision. In Iraq, he had dared to go further and faster to transform US foreign policy from multilateral diplomacy to aggressive unilateral militarism. Likewise, he went further and faster in widening the domestic gap between rich and poor, a daring demolition of what remained of the New Deal welfare state. These goals were popular with most rich Americans from 2000 through 2004. Moreover, 9/11 gave Bush the political cover and capital to pursue these goals further and faster. But as 9/11 receded into history, Bush's pursuit produced a predictable backlash.

The war and occupation provoked violent resistance inside Iraq that the US could not contain. More importantly, it increased political, diplomatic, and ideological opposition to the US nearly everywhere. As the war dragged on and its costs rose, so too did criticism. Beyond harsh denunciations of that criticism, Bush moved to prevent potential domestic opposition by curtailing civil liberties and expanding federal power to wage an endless war against terrorism. The transformation of US foreign policy into a military unilateralism thus took on higher costs (political, cultural, as well as economic; foreign and domestic) than rich Americans (as well as others) were content to pay. They wanted US foreign interests to be advanced, but more slowly, multilaterally, and diplomatically than the Bush-Cheney-Rumsfeld approach.

Much the same happened to the Bush economic policies (tax changes, relaxed industrial regulations, cheap labor immigration, subsidies to favored industries, encouragement of job outsourcing, and so on). Together such policies accelerated the declining conditions of most middle- and lower-income families. Increasingly stressed by longer and harder work and mounting debts, those families had begun to complain about, criticize, and oppose Bush policies. The richest Americans had benefited from Bush economics far more than the rest of the population, as widening wealth and income disparities showed. Rumblings of mass discontent made many of the richest Americans determined somehow to soften and slow the Bush economic program. Otherwise it might be ended or, worse still, reversed.

The elections of 2006 may thus continue the basic Bush shifts in foreign policy and domestic economic change but less quickly, less sharply, less offensively. The elections weakened the Bush approach and removed some of its most aggressive leaders (e.g., Rumsfeld). The elections empowered Democrats to slow and soften Bush policies and thereby hopefully to reduce opposition to them. The richest Americans' votes and contributions to Democrats represented their demand that the Bush program be drastically moderated. Bush, his cabinet, and their neo-con gurus were not trusted to achieve the required moderation quickly (even the James A. Baker III-Lee Hamilton commission redesigning Iraq policy was too slow, too little, and too late). Many of America's richest concluded that financing and voting for Democrats was necessary.

Bush and "his" Republicans had gone far to reconstitute a pre-1929 kind of US capitalism and to reposition the US as the world's dominant unilateralist military power as well as economic center. But en route to these welcomed gains, they had overshot the mark in ways deemed dangerous by many of the richest Americans. Thus, they turned to the Democrats to mollify all those offended, frightened, or damaged by Bush's programs while consolidating and solidifying those same programs' achievements. The classical oscillation between the two parties should once again serve the system and its chief beneficiaries that finance them both. Republicans can console themselves with the knowledge that, once the Democrats have done their job, Republicans can reasonably expect America's richest to switch back and support their approach yet again.

Real Costs of Executives' Money Grabs

28 December 2006

Goldman Sachs, the investment bank, paid out over $16 billion in 2006 "bonuses" to its employees, with over $50 million going to its chairman alone. Pfizer, the drug company, paid a "severance package" of $200 million to its just-resigned chief executive. Many other large corporations acted similarly. All this is legal, given the laws and rules that corporations win from their political allies. Indeed, the latest ruling by the Securities and Exchange Commission (SEC) allows corporations to obscure what they pay top executives—"a victory for corporations," the *New York Times* called it (27 December 2006: C1).

The real costs of such executive payouts are immense. One such cost is suggested by what the executives themselves say when they explain their opposition to workers' wage increases. Then they argue that, if wages were raised, it would inevitably require the prices of what those workers produce to also rise, thereby hurting consumers in the end. The executives position themselves as guardians of consumers' interests against the workers' "unreasonable demands" for wage increases. If one accepts this logic, it must then apply as well to executives' pay packages. The billions paid out to executives will likewise "inevitably require prices to rise." Put simply, the companies that pay billions to top executives will do everything they can to recoup those payouts by charging more to their customers and thus ultimately to consumers. We all pay for those executives' money grabs.

Yet we pay in more ways than just higher prices. When the companies that hire an investment bank like Goldman Sachs have to pay huge fees (needed to enable the "bonuses"), it hurts those companies' profits. They will respond by trying not only to raise their prices to consumers but also to save on their other costs. Similarly, companies like Pfizer will try to offset the cost of their huge executive payouts by not only raising their prices but also saving on their production costs. Cost reductions have been achieved by shifting from full to part-time work, from regular to "temp" employees, from union to non-union work-forces, and from US to foreign workers. Thus, high executive payouts mean, for most of the rest of us, lower incomes and fewer jobs as well as higher prices.

We also suffer the consequences of high executive payouts in still other ways. The billions paid out by corporations in bonuses and severance packages for top executives are billions not spent on other things. For example, those billions could have been spent to improve technology, invent new products, provide training to raise workers' productivity, and in other ways grow these corporations and make them more globally competitive. One reason why most capitalist corporations in other countries do not pay their executives as much as US corporations do is that they are more focused on competitive growth. In the long run, such trends also threaten US workers as a whole.

The costs of huge executive payouts are neither corrected nor compensated by our political system, as the SEC decision mentioned above shows. Where once the top income tax bracket—that affected chiefly the sorts of huge incomes now grabbed by executives—was 91 percent, in recent decades it has been more like 35 percent. The rich got the tax laws changed to allow them to keep more of the payouts they arrange for themselves. Changed tax laws have thus been an immense incentive for executives to grab as much as possible now before mass opposition might once again drive the top tax brackets back up to where they once were.

The executives learned from US history. In the final decades of the nineteenth century, leaders of corporations took huge payouts to establish huge fortunes. One reaction was the passage of an income tax law in 1910 aimed exclusively at only the richest Americans. Those richest Americans quickly developed a counter-strategy to change the new income tax law.

They succeeded and thereby spread the burden of the income tax across the entire population, which eventually undermined popular support for the income tax. In a burst of income-tax opposition around the time of Reagan's presidency, the richest Americans got another tax-law change—tax cuts—giving them by far the biggest tax break. And so, very predictably, the zoom-up in executive pay packages took off to reach the record 2006 numbers.

All of which makes one wonder which of the following three scenarios will best describe what happens in the next few years. Perhaps the divisions separating the rich from the middle and poor will expand even further, with all the social consequences that flow from growing inequalities. It is worth pondering the implications of having 15 million Americans who earned the minimum wage of $5.15 per hour for 40 hours per week in 2006 struggling alongside the $53.4 million "bonus" of Lloyd Blankfein, the Goldman Sachs chairman, which works out to be over $25,000 per hour for his 40 hours per week (*New York Times*, 24 December 2006). As a second possibility, the Democratic gains last November might revive demands to limit executive grabs by new tax and other laws. As a third conceivable scenario, Americans may learn from history to suspect that a new set of laws will be as easily undone or evaded by corporations and their executives as the last set was. Then they will have to consider more basic changes in how enterprises are organized and run, who makes the basic decisions, and what are the ultimate goals for the production of goods and services and the incomes generated from that production.

The Decline of Public Higher Education

17 February 2007

Over the last quarter century, Americans got used to the idea of their children going on to colleges and universities. In the early 1970s, about 8.5 million Americans attended such institutions; by 2004 the number had doubled. The US population across this time rose by less than 50 percent. This spectacular growth in our student population reflected the pent-up demand of the mass of Americans for what they had viewed as a luxury as well as a ticket to better jobs and higher incomes. The demand would have far exceeded the supply had not most of the states rapidly increased facilities for public higher education. Today, the vast majority of US college and university students attend public, not private, institutions. Yet therein lies precisely the problem.

The last quarter century, and especially the last decade, have also moved the country rightward towards less government provision of social services (like public higher education) and more privatization. Real wages have stagnated since the 1970s, so most Americans are finding it ever more difficult to pay for public higher education. Meanwhile its costs have been rising far faster than the general level of inflation. We are on a collision course in which a historic demand for higher education—which has now become an embedded expectation for half the population—confronts a rapidly escalating rationing of enrollment by cost. Social tensions and rising resentment and anger are sure to follow.

Let's take the example of the main campus of a major state university: the University of Massachusetts at Amherst. Approximately 25,000 students, undergraduate and graduate, attend that university. About three quarters come from Massachusetts households. The total cost for in-state undergraduate students went from $2,340 in 1978–79 to $16,584 this academic year. That increase was three times as big as the rise in the consumer price index over the same period. The increase was larger still for out-of-state undergraduates. Given that real wages stagnated across this period, paying for their children's college-level education presented families with an ever-rising level of financial difficulty. No wonder the data shows that American workers over the last 25 years steadily increased the number of hours worked per year (multiple jobs and/or more overtime). No wonder those families increased household debt at historically unprecedented rates to historically unprecedented levels.

Nor is it any wonder that students now graduating US colleges and universities do so with increasing levels of personal debt (in addition to their parents' household debt) taken to pay part of college costs. The US Department of Education says that in 2004–2005, two thirds of students graduated from colleges and universities with debt (averaging $15,500 at public schools and $20,000 at private schools). In New York, which runs the nation's largest system of public higher education, the average debt was $21,000 then, and it is higher today.

Several lessons flow from this situation. First, many parents have reacted strongly to the additional stress and exhaustion (from the increasing hours of paid work they have undertaken) and the additional debt anxieties (from the fast rising levels of household debt) incurred since the early 1970s to finance runaway college costs. Some have turned against higher education in a deepening rage about the financial burdens that it imposes. This can take the form of hostility toward teachers and teachers' salaries in so far as these are blamed for rising college costs. It can take the form of a cultural turn against higher education: viewed increasingly as an unnecessary and useless distraction from "real" life and a job or as a luxury indulgence for the idle or both. Most likely, anger about college costs will flow into the growing "middle-class malaise" that fuels the rhetoric and campaigns of many Democrats and mystifies so many Republicans (at least, those who don't simply deny it or its basis in hard realities).

Nor have matters been improved as public universities, to save costs, resort ever more to substituting overworked and underpaid "adjuncts" for the full-time tenured faculty who used to do most of the teaching. New PhDs face ever fewer tenure-track jobs and so must take multiple adjunct positions at different institutions. They have far less time for each class and little or no time for the research that should enable them to keep up with their discipline and improve their teaching across their working life. Grossly underpaid in comparison to what tenure-track teachers get, they resent their situation. Rising pressures not matched by rising resources, respect, or remuneration also provoke more dissatisfaction and resentment among the relatively shrinking portion of tenured professors. The deteriorating circumstances of the teachers spill over to diminish the educational experiences of the students. The students have thus been required to pay ever more for ever less in the way of educational services. What keeps students in school is the terror of facing a deteriorating job market without a degree. They remain students despite the quality of their classroom experiences.

Nothing better illustrates all these trends than the current rapid proliferation of "distance-learning"—the prevailing euphemism for internet-based courses. In them, very low-paid adjuncts administer electronic courses that students increasingly substitute for the formerly in-person engagement with tenured professors. In many state universities, faculty reductions have so limited classes that undergraduates find it necessary to add an extra semester or two (and its heavy costs) to get sufficient classes to graduate in their chosen major fields. Offering such students "distance-learning" via the internet is proving a profitable new opportunity for such universities.

The finance-driven turn to adjuncts and distance learning widens the gulf between public and private higher education. The private colleges and universities see the decline of public colleges and universities as a competitive opportunity in the business sense. The democratization of higher education had been notably advanced after World War II when the states built up first-rate institutions that often outperformed the best and oldest private institutions. Now, that short-lived democratization is unraveling and with it the quality of higher education provided to the majority of our students. A differentiation of first-class (private) and second-class (public) higher education is hardening into the norm with many state and community colleges sinking further into still lower quality educational experiences. It would be hard to exaggerate the complex consequences of these developments for many years and in many domains of our society.

Reversing the American Dream

24 February 2007

Industry officials expect around 120,000 reverse mortgages to be signed in 2007. In 1990, only 150 reverse mortgages were arranged. In reverse mortgages, people who already own their homes borrow from lenders (receiving lump sums and/or monthly payments and/or lines of credit); in return, the lenders then acquire rising equity in those homes. Eventually such borrowers or their heirs must sell the home to repay the principal and accumulated interest. Traditional mortgages were the opposite: borrowing homebuyers repaid lenders principal plus interest over many years to build up their home equity, to become genuine owners of their homes. They allowed millions of American families, especially after World War II, to change from tenants to homeowners, thereby realizing what came to be known as the American Dream.

Today's reverse mortgages are a new means for liquidating that dream. They would better be described as "wealth-transfer" than "wealth-management" tools.

Tens of thousands of Americans aged 62 (the legally mandated minimum age for eligibility) or more are now receiving monthly reverse-mortgage payments. They will get them for some or all of the rest of their lives. In this way, they can supplement the inadequate Social Security and often modest pension or investment income they must depend upon after retirement.

As all statistics show, the only significant asset that Americans accumulate during their working years is their home. The economic realities of our times now require that people draw down that asset via reverse mortgages to fund their post-retirement years. They will thus not leave their homes to their children. Meanwhile the mass refinancing of home mortgages by Americans during their working years is also reducing their home equity as they approach retirement.

The combination of refinancing and reverse mortgages is quickly eroding the historically short-lived period of mass home ownership in the US.

The National Reverse Mortgage Lenders Association (NRMLA) reports that its member lenders grew from 370 in 2005 to over 500 in 2006. Their business has been booming across the country. The percentage increases in numbers of reverse mortgages signed from 2005 to 2006 were 71.4 percent in New York City, 97.1 percent in Boston, 157.9 percent in Coral Gables, and 238.6 percent in Phoenix. Such growth rates result partly because sizeable origination fees and interest charges on such loans make them particularly attractive for lenders.

However, the main reason is the rising home prices of recent years. They provided the only positive economic reality for millions of Americans whose security portfolios, if any, have been in tough shape since 2000, and whose pensions and health benefits (current and future) have been reduced or threatened with reduction. As the negative realities increasingly eat into the cash flows of the fast-rising portion of the population reaching 62, they discover in reverse mortgages a solution for improving that cash flow. In the smooth yet expectant rhetoric of Peter Bell, president of the NRMLA, "More seniors are recognizing that traditional retirements tools, such as IRAs, pensions and 401(k)s are not providing sufficient income to help fund everyday living expenses and healthcare."

No data exist on how many seniors choose reverse mortgages to avoid burdening their children for ongoing support in their final years. Likewise no data exists on how many of those children will not discover the cost of reverse mortgages until their parents' estate is debited to repay the reverse mortgage lender. Yet we know the importance of home ownership to Americans' sense of well-being. Sociologists and psychologists have demonstrated the widespread expectation that children will inherit their parents' homes and be homeowners themselves. Thus, the social effects, if reverse mortgages continue to soar, are likely to be profound. To paraphrase poet Langston Hughes, a dream deferred is a dangerous thing, and a dream erased is worse.

Old Distributions, New Economy

with Max Fraad-Wolff

16 April 2007

T he macro march backward of domestic income and wealth distribution has become remarkable. At least we thought so enough to pen the following remarks. In 2006 the corporate profits share of the national economy retouched its 1929 high. Wage and salary income broke its eight-decade low watermark. Our new economy increasingly replicates the distributional landscape of the late 19th and early 20th centuries. Nowhere is this more clearly demonstrated than in the relation of taxes and income of the richest among us. In their widely published research, Parisian professor Thomas Piketty and his colleague at UC Berkeley, Professor Emmanuel Saez, have documented how far the progressiveness of the federal income tax has collapsed. The Center on Budget and Policy Priorities (CBPP) in Washington has also further developed the research.[1]

Thus the effective tax rates on the highest income earners (the top 1 percent of taxpayers) fell from a range of 45–75 percent in the early 1970s to a range of 30–35 percent in 2004. Over the same period, the tax rate for the middle fifth of the income distribution barely changed. Both Democratic and Republican presidents and Congresses presided over these trends. Debt has kept the realities of our internet-enabled, cutting-edge, early-20th-century economy from being widely understood. The Federal Government borrows back from the rich the taxes it no longer collects from them so it can keep spending freely. Toiling multitudes follow suit. They borrow the wages they didn't get and then some. Thus, consumption booms to 70 percent of GDP as wages fall as a percentage of our overall economy.

While the top 1 percent of income-earning households in the US saw their income tax rate drop so sharply from 1970 to 2004, this same top 1 percent saw the portion of total US pre-tax income they received rise from around 10 percent in 1970 to over 17 percent in 2004. For the people living in the roughly

1 million households that comprise this top 1 percent, the economic news has never been better. The highest shelf cashes in on our cycles of assets appreciation. These are the private investors who performed best during the long stock market and real estate booms (1982–2000, 2003–2007). Wealth is increasingly top-heavy in distribution and generative of higher income than labor. The rest of the US income distribution sinks deeper into personal debt. Great monies were made loaning ever more to them. As incomes stagnate and liabilities soar, asset bubbles sustain dreams and schemes. We have become a land of Wal-Mart and Net Jets where everyone thinks he is in the middle class. Everyone, that is, who is yet to file for our new and improved bankruptcy.

The US economy is still very much caught up in the shifts and adjustments connected to large and sustained changes in distribution of income and tax burden. Trying to hold on to rising standards of living, expected as birthright, households face a permanent cash flow crisis as 150 years of rising real wages (decade over decade) ended with stagnation since the 1970s. How could rising consumption continue without rising wages? Households' taxes were never significantly reduced, so reduced taxes could not fund consumption.

In round one, America sent more household members (especially women) out to work. This has morphed into sending all household members to do more labor (shifting from part-time to full-time and taking second jobs). When that proved insufficient, taking on personal debt (home mortgages, home equity lines of credit, 5-year auto loans, credit-card debt) exploded. Flat wages, globalization, and financial engineering economically make over and hide deepening lines and failing health. The ride has been spectacular, and may not be over yet.

As debt rises and earnings stagnate, savings go negative. The US had a net negative savings rate over the last year. Where does all the credit come from? Global financial deregulation and rising fragility in financial intermediaries frame the answer. The cheap cash from heavy savings in East Asia and petroleum exporter windfalls finds its way to American consumers. Thus, the IMF reports that, in 2006, the US borrowed 65 percent of the world's available savings. We generate about 22 percent of global GDP and have 5 percent of the earth's population. It would seem that our debt and private consumption have moved out of sustainable alignment. This has been partially and temporarily remedied by innovations in debt repackaging and risk sharing. Securitization of debt and derivatives allow for endless repackaging and default risk transfer in rapidly growing speculative and hedging product markets. Thus, the unsustainable becomes routine, profitable, and manageable.

The "collapse of the middle" in the income distribution will likely continue as will the changed burden of taxes. As long as debt levels, delusional understandings, and ready lies from officials oblige. Closed eyes will shield people from reality. Producers, importers, wholesalers, and retailers who miss this process will suffer reverses. Entrepreneurs who see the overall picture evolving will identify the new opportunities. Sadly, the public seems to think that government regulation is their best bet. It would appear they, as well as many liberal commentators, are unaware that the upward redistributions they resent are largely the fruit of government policy shifts.

As the public begins to grasp the precariousness of its position, however, we expect violent attitude realignments. The rapid drop in support for globalization and President Bush's slide from grace will appear slow in comparison to future swings in opinion that we anticipate will be fierce and fast.

---

1 Thomas Piketty and Emmanuel Saez, "How Progressive Is the U.S. Federal Tax System? A Historical and International Perspective," *Journal of Economic Perspectives*, Winter 2007. Thomas Piketty is a professor of economics at the Paris School of Economics. Emmanuel Saez is a professor of economics at the University of California, Berkeley. This analysis also relies on data the authors made available on the web: elsa.berkeley.edu/~saez/jep-results-standalone.xls. See also Aviva Aron-Dine, writing on the website (29 March 2007) of Center on Budget and Policy Priorities: www.cbpp.org/3-29-07tax.htm.

Today's Haunting Specter, or What Needs Doing

6 June 2007

An attractive social democrat, Ségolène Royal, just lost the French presidential race to a neoliberal candidate, leaving French leftists debating the causes of their failures and what to do about them. The center-left in Italy recently defeated the staunch neoliberal, Silvio Berlusconi. Yet its incapacities to define a new and different social program or mobilize mass support for it leave Italian leftists debating the same basic issues as the French. Talking to Europeans (as I did this last month) exposes the mix of strategic confusion and general demoralization that now haunts the broad left nearly everywhere.

One central issue is a lack of conviction among leftists about resuming the old programs of welfare-focused state interventions that neoliberalism has everywhere more or less dismantled. Thus some (like Blair, Clinton, et al.) move to reduce (or, as often marketed, to "modernize") those programs. Others doggedly keep advocating the classic mix of welfare state-interventionist programs anyway, but without enthusiasm. Electorates sense these ambivalences among social democrats and often compare them unfavorably with the self-confidence of global neoliberalism's advocates. Neoliberalism won sufficient mass support to become hegemonic by attacking welfare state programs and the regimes implementing them for their evident failures to solve serious social problems. Privatization and free markets were heavily advertised as the better solutions.

When neoliberal spokespersons attacked social democracy's failures they found ready audiences. These included the workers who discovered that the jobs, wages, and social benefits—won by the broad left in the aftermath of the Great Depression—could not subsequently be secured by left parties (in or out of power). Also receptive were many former students caught up in the tumultuous 1960s. They learned then that left parties either could not or would not match their actions to their rhetoric about equality and solidarity even when mass support for doing so had been mobilized. And, of course, neoliberalism won most of the right and center-right political formations that had been frightened and angered by the left turns produced by the Depression and intensified in the 1960s. They were eager to reverse those turns.

Neoliberalism's mass supporters are increasingly disappointed by its actual results: another case where "truth in advertising" has not been enforced. But they will not switch back toward a social democracy that was so recently and massively disappointing as well—and especially not when it is advocated so ambivalently. Thus the left in today's advanced industrial capitalisms seems disorganized, demoralized, rudderless, and unfocused. With no compelling vision or program, it wallows in weak "oppositional" reactions to neoliberalism's continuing initiatives.

This sorry situation will not change unless and until the left answers two key questions. First, why did past social democratic achievements prove insecure in the face of neoliberalism's attacks? Second, what kind of new social democratic vision and program could mobilize the left and win mass support to resume change in the direction of genuine economic and social equality, democracy, and solidarity? So here are some thoughts, based on recent interviews in Europe, to add to our efforts to answer these questions.

In the past, social democracy called for using the state to offset, correct, regulate, and otherwise manage the workings of capitalism. It sought a capitalism with a human face: one with fewer inequalities of wealth, income, power, and access to culture. The state was to manage capital investment, regulate markets, and shape the distribution of income and wealth: all in the interest of a society with a deeper and more widely shared sense of community. Economic growth and efficiency, attributed to capitalism, were to be supported while state policy would prevent or counteract the socially undesirable consequences of private capitalist production and commodity markets. State interventionist capitalism was the solution; private capitalism free of state controls and interventions was the problem.

The social democratic solution thus constrained what private capitalists could do in their profit-driven competition with one another and their profit-driven relations with employees and customers. *But it left them in the position of receiving and dispensing enterprise profits.* Social democracy thus left private capitalists with the incentive to weaken, deflect, or remove those constraints. It also provided capitalists with the means—their retained profits—to do so. In a sense, this was the historic capitalist-socialist compromise of the 19th and 20th centuries. Capitalists could keep their positions as receivers and dispensers of enterprise profits, but the conditions of those positions would be constrained by social(ist) welfare state policies.

Whatever its benefits, this historic compromise set the stage for new struggles. Welfare states became contested terrains: social democrats sought to strengthen and expand them, while capitalists sought to reduce, weaken, or eliminate them. From the 1930s to the early 1970s, despite some social democratic gains, the trend moved in the direction that favored capitalists. The trend turned into a rout in the 1970s and has remained so ever since. The capitalists used their profits to improve their business prospects and performance by, among other strategies, undoing welfare statism. By lobbying, moving production outside national borders, immigration, common markets, media campaigns, and countless other mechanisms, the capitalists succeeded in bringing social democracy to its current sorry state.

Even where trade unions and socialist and communist parties were strong, they proved no match for the profits capitalists could use against them. Moreover, the capitalists eventually grasped that capturing the mass imagination was the most effective weapon in their arsenal, less costly and socially disruptive than direct confrontations in parliaments or factories or schools or in the streets. Nor could social democrats advocate the obvious, namely that the capitalists be deprived of their profits and thus their chief means to fight social democracy.

The Cold War blocked such advocacy. In the USSR, private capitalists had been eliminated in industrial enterprises and replaced by state officials. Demonizing the Soviets generally worked nicely in advanced industrial capitalisms to dissuade social democrats there from demanding any similar replacement of private capitalists. Moreover, although few social democrats grasped this even after 1989, the Soviet revolution of 1917 had in effect replaced private capitalists with state-appointed capitalists. Workers in Soviet industrial enterprises, like their counterparts in private capitalist enterprises, still produced profits *for others*. Instead of private boards of directors, Soviet commissars did the "appropriation and distribution of the surpluses" as Marx put it. Industrial workers never became the appropriators and distributors of the surpluses ("profits") they produced. Thus, when Soviet industry foundered in a major crisis in the 1980s, those commissars could quite easily re-privatize industry and "neoliberalize" post-Soviet society. As commissars they utilized the surpluses they received from Soviet workers to accomplish the re-privatization of Soviet state industry. Then, as private capitalists, they utilized their profits to impose shock-therapy neoliberalism. And just as elsewhere, Russians disappointed with neoliberalism's results there are not about to switch back to the deeply discredited Soviet alternative.

The new direction and strategy for social democracy follows from the flaw in its historic compromise with capitalism. The egalitarian, solidary society envisioned by social democracy cannot be secured so long as a group of people with the incentives and means to prevent it are left in place. A transformation of the structure of production inside each enterprise could change the basic situation in so far as it ended the dichotomy between workers and capitalists. The collective of workers that produces the surplus/profits would become the same collective that appropriates and distributes the surplus/profits. Full participation in work and its products would then make possible and foster full participation in political democracy and cultural activity. Achieving this fundamental reorganization of each enterprise must become a core policy of social democracy.

Instead of old social democratic policies inadequate to their goals, this projected transformation of the structure and practice of all work represents a dramatic new vision and program. It offers the basis on and with which to construct an egalitarian, solidary society. Advocacy of such a program might reanimate, unify, and focus the forces of a new left today.

Twenty Years of Widening Inequality

1 November 2007

The Internal Revenue Service tracks the incomes of Americans as recorded in their tax returns each year. The latest numbers, covering 1986 to 2005, summarize one basic feature of this country's evolving economy and politics: the sharply widening gap between haves and have-nots. Consider the richest 1 percent of Americans. They filed 1.3 million tax returns in 2005 reporting an average of $1.2 million of "adjusted gross income" (AGI) per tax return for that year. Together this 1 percent of Americans took in 21.2 percent of the total AGI earned by all Americans. Back in 1986, the richest 1 percent took in half as big a chunk of the nation's income—"only" 11.3 percent of total AGI.

The richest million Americans in the US got very much richer than everyone else over the last twenty years. Their ballooning share of the nation's income was *both* cause and result of downsizing many corporate and government payrolls, depressing real wages, deregulation, neoliberalism, globalization, and the rest of the agenda shared by big business, most Republicans, and most Democrats. The basic social deal had two sides. The richest 1 percent provides the big bucks for political campaigns and candidates: from their own pockets and from the profits of their businesses. In return, federal, state, and local governments outdid one another in deregulating business (especially the biggest), helping US firms (especially the biggest) expand globally, and reducing taxes on business (especially the biggest) and the rich (especially the richest). The two parties competed for contributions from the rich by promising, if elected, to secure or expand the laws and government practices that had made them rich.

At the other end of the income distribution, the bottom 75 percent of households—the overwhelming majority—shared 37.5 percent of the total national AGI in 2005. The last twenty years were not good for them; in 1986 they together had 41 percent. While this majority got a smaller share of the total income to support its interests, the top 1 percent nearly doubled the share it could use to support its interests. Millions in the majority lost secure jobs with benefits and had to take multiple, precarious positions with less or no benefits. Their real weekly wages fell. Their families sent more members out to work more jobs, and they borrowed vast sums against their homes and on their credit cards. The last twenty years strained their households, relationships, and family values with massive infusions of exhaustion, job stress, and debt anxiety. They shifted consumption from Sears and Macy's to Wal-Mart. Many lost interest in civic participation, in following current events, in the Democrats, and even in the minimalist act of voting. People seemed incapable or unwilling to stop the developments that were putting them under such economic, social, and personal pressures.

Meanwhile, the super-rich 1 percent were having quite the opposite experience. They took an increasing interest in politics. Ever more millionaires and billionaires ran for offices. Their contributions often determined which candidates won party primaries. Their potential enmity cautioned every incumbent to serve their interests (or risk being replaced by those who would) and thereby receive their largesse. In the economy, the top 1 percent enjoyed the massive shift of production toward them. Profits rose fastest for those enterprises that produced the most expensive housing, vacations, transportation, restaurants, and clothing. The lavish spending of the rich became the ever more pervasive cultural icon. The masses shifted to buy at Wal-Mart, while the top 1 percent's stock portfolios added Wal-Mart shares. Nothing better illustrated the linkages between the bottom and the top. The mounting distresses of the former provided yet more profit opportunities for the latter.

Between the haves and the have-nots, there are always some "think-they-haves." Many of them exist among those with incomes lower than the top 1 percent but higher than the bottom 75 percent. They are the upper echelons of those who serve the top. This quarter of the population saw little change in the share of total national income flowing into their hands between 1986 and 2005. Instead, with mounting nervousness they watched the decline of the bottom 75 percent and with admiring envy the consumption orgies and political self-promotions of the super rich. The think-they-haves borrowed their way up to taste the lifestyles of the top 1 percent, pressed their children to aspire to a good hedge fund job, and comforted one another with assurances that rising incomes and home prices would assuredly keep them solvent despite mounting debts.

Rumbling ominously beneath the new century's widening income inequalities are fissures likewise widening. The hedge funds' wild profits—which made so many of the top 1 percent so rich—required pushing mortgages on those too squeezed at the bottom to make their monthly payments. Global and US deregulations fostered rose-colored over-valuations by rating companies of the new securities backed by these questionable mortgages. Thus, the new super rich in the US made billions by palming off unsafe securities on their counterparts across the globe. Now, as the super rich everywhere seek to escape from the deluge of losses and recrimination as their unsafe investments collapse, the house of cards they constructed trembles.

The arrival of new aspirants (in China, India, and so on)—wanting entry to the top 1 percent—also shook the world. It created additional resource demands—from the world's mines, lands, oil and gas wells, food and water supplies, and much else. Discovery, exploitation, and competition for scarce resources became more urgent and desperate. The new aspirants wanted to change or else disengage from and so undermine the old global economic arrangements built on existing markets, the World Bank, and the IMF and favoring above all the central role of the US economy and its currency.

Twenty years of mounting inequality continues to produce major social changes, major population movements, and major national and international conflicts. Diverse groupings of people seek to cope with, survive, or profit from rapid as well as profound change. What trend might the widening income inequality in the US portend in the global context? A global top 1 percent and its attendant top 25 percent of upper echelon servants are emerging, seeking to get into a position like that of their counterparts in the US. That may spell a relative decline of the lower 75 percent of the US distribution. Raising the top quarter of the global income distribution toward US standards may very well cost the bottom 75 percent of the US income distribution a deterioration toward global standards.

Neoliberalism in Globalized Trouble

4 December 2007

Wild stock market gyrations and a global financial melt-down open 2008. Around the world, old and new critics of neoliberalism smirk and repeat "I told you so." Neoliberal dogma—that private enterprise is good and efficient whereas state economic interventions are bad and wasteful—suffers deepening disrepute. The private, deregulated capitalism of recent decades produced imprudent credit orgies that generated unsustainable bubbles bursting across scary headlines. The final straw broke in the world's biggest private banks, especially those in the US. Those financial hustlers had packaged loans into securities to which they attached hyped credit ratings (purchased from other private enterprises). They then sold the securities to the gullible and greedy (often other nations' bankers and state officials).

This latest private profit-driven bubble deflated once the reality of debts that could not be repaid revealed the inflated credit ratings. Huge financial losses and evaporating credit spread anxiety. How many businesses will fail, how many jobs will be lost, how many government programs will get cut as tax revenues fall, and how long will this last? Global capitalist efficiency is giving us yet another recession. Despite hunger, homelessness, joblessness, and poverty, businesses produce less because credit has dried up. Rising unemployment reduces purchases, which in turn deepens unemployment in a vicious cycle. Reduced state services coincide with the rising need for them. The human and material waste, the irrationality, and the inefficiency of recession proliferate. Because those with the most resources can best cushion the negative impacts, economic and social injustices worsen.

Panicked bankers and politicians around the world temporarily abandon neoliberal beliefs. They want the government to compensate for and help to fix the economic disasters. As always, this is to be done by using public tax monies to solve the problems without constraining, let alone punishing, private capitalism for the mess it produced.

Two groups of critics focus on neoliberalism's troubles these days. The first group includes all the old devotees of Keynesianism, the welfare state, and the idea that government regulation can and should save capitalism from its own self-destructive excesses. They welcome the latest statements by leaders of the Federal Reserve, the Congress, and even this president as they finally recognize the current economic dangers. They applaud plans for government intervention to "correct" and "solve" the problems of private capitalism. Another New Deal is their ideal of what is needed.

The second group disagrees with the first. For them, the New Deal is a "been there, done that" to which they add, "and that was nowhere near enough." They point out that while the New Deal imposed rules and regulations on private businesses, it always left the private capitalists in their position of receiving and disposing of profits. That position gave them the incentive and the resources to evade and eventually to undermine the New Deal government controls. They practiced evasion from the 1930s to the 1970s. After that, they and their agents (Reagan, Bush, Clinton, and Bush) openly dismantled the welfare state. They did this in the name of the superior economic efficiency, growth, and prosperity claimed to flow from free, unregulated, private capitalist enterprise.

The first group wants Clinton, Obama, McCain, or whoever wins to renew the business-regulating welfare state and thereby fix a broken private capitalism whose mass public support is dwindling. That program, they insist, is the only "realistic" solution to the current crisis. They dismiss the second group for offering programs that are socially divisive and dangerous, unrealizable utopian fantasies.

The second group mocks the "realism" of the first group. The New Deal's "realism" left capitalists in the position to undo the New Deal, which they did. To repeat that mistake now is not realistic, they say; it is absurd. To secure society against the inefficiencies of private capitalism requires that capitalists stop occupying the position of receiver and distributer of society's profits. Instead, this second group insists, the workers themselves must take that position.

As neoliberalism unravels, critical opposition to capitalism's social failures and mounting costs everywhere splits into these two groups. This replicates the critical opposition that earlier rose against slavery and feudalism when their times in history ended. On the one hand, some of those critics wanted better working and living conditions for slaves and serfs; they demanded state intervention to impose those conditions. However, other critics disagreed and said that improved treatment for slaves and serfs would never be secure so long as slavery and feudalism continued. This group said the basic problems were slavery and feudalism as intolerable social systems. So they fought for—and eventually won—their abolition.

Today, critics' calls for a renewal of the old welfare state and for government regulation and control over private business are increasing globally. But the other group of critics is also gaining. In Germany, for example, the Left Party (*Die Linke*) is moving, albeit gingerly, beyond classical welfare statism toward more radical responses to neoliberalism's current crisis. The focus is becoming capitalism per se as the ruling social system that ought to be abolished.

The big issue for this group is what to propose in capitalism's place. The chief lessons learned from actually existing socialisms in the twentieth century concern what *not* to do. The state and state economic intervention are thus no longer viewed as the solutions for the wastes and injustices of private capitalism. Instead, this group aims to change the economic base, the system of production itself. This means empowering and repositioning workers so that their jobs include receiving and distributing the profits their work yields. Their goal: to dissolve the distinction of worker and boss much as the earlier distinctions of master and slave, feudal lord and serf were overcome.

Today's global crisis of neoliberalism is propelling this last, radical group into the public arena. More from them will surely be heard in the years ahead.

Evading Taxes, Legally

25 February 2008

Clever public relations make millions believe that taxes are "too high," as if all citizens and all businesses were in the same boat when it comes to paying taxes. Actually, we are in different boats, some sailing, some stalled, and some sinking. Taxes on some of us are indeed high or too high, but others of "us" enjoy low or no taxes.

Taxes on property show this all too clearly. Cities and towns across this country rely heavily on taxing chiefly land, buildings (homes, stores, factories, and office buildings), and vehicles. This kind of property is called *tangible* property. However another kind of property, called *intangible*, is almost never taxed, not by cities and towns nor by states or the federal government. Intangible property includes stocks, bonds, cash, accounts receivable, and so on.

For example, suppose you own two houses in the US, each worth $300,000. You must pay a property tax on each house to the town(s) where they are located. However, if you sell one house and invest the $300,000 proceeds in stocks or bonds, you pay NO property tax on those stocks or bonds. In short, for those rich enough to own significant quantities of stocks and bonds, that intangible property is not subject to property taxation. How very nice for them.

Keep in mind the difference between property taxes and income taxes. The *income* earned from tangible property (like rent from land or houses) is taxable, just like the *income* from intangible property (like dividends and interest). But the property itself is taxable only if it is tangible and not if it is intangible. Tangible property that produces income to its owner is thus taxed twice (on the value of the property *and* on the income from the property), while intangible property pays tax only once (on the income from it, not on the property's value).

The total value of just stocks and bonds in the US amounts to many trillions of dollars of currently untaxed intangible property. A very low tax rate could raise a great deal of money for federal, state, and local governments, more than enough to allow other taxes to fall and government spending on social programs to rise or both. How low a rate? An answer emerges from some rare, recent experiences with intangible property taxes in the US. Americans of courage and principle have sometimes taxed intangible property.

Kentucky is one of very few states currently taxing intangible property. It levies 1.5 cents per $100 on businesses' accounts receivable and certain other "intangible property rights." In 1931, the state of Florida passed a law imposing a property tax on common stocks. After a lobbying effort of eight years, in August 2006 Governor Jeb Bush proudly signed the repeal of that 1931 law. In its last year, the law brought the state of Florida $130 million in tax revenues. All Floridians with more than $370,000 in stocks were required to pay. Those with intangible property worth less that $370,001 were exempt. In its last year, 180,000 Floridians paid property taxes on intangible property they owned. Given the state's population then of approximately 18 million people, that works out to 1 percent of Floridians who paid intangible property taxes. The tax fell on those most able to pay—and only on them— which is why their man Bush worked so hard to kill it.

Governor Bush's explanations for his effort did not improve his family's reputation for smarts. He denounced the state's intangible property tax for "penalizing those who chose to work, save and invest." The good governor probably forgot that his constant support for tangible property taxes continually penalizes those who chose to work, save, and invest in land or homes or local stores, office buildings, and factories in Florida.

Florida legislators who voted to repeal the tax on intangibles justified their action by arguing that rich Floridians could and did legally transfer their intangible property out of Florida to escape the taxes. In short, the legislators used the fact of tax evasion not to tighten the intangible property tax laws.

Instead, they pointed to evasion of the property tax law as a reason to repeal the law. How very nice for Florida's wealthiest.

A tax on intangible property would work best at the federal level. That way, moving assets from one state to another would provide no tax evasion. The current technology of tracking stock and bond transactions, the requirement to list income from intangible property on existing IRS tax returns, and tax law agreements between the US and other countries would do much to prevent tax evasion by moving intangible wealth abroad. Tax evasion is, after all, a problem for all types of taxes levied in the US (as in other countries). It is hardly a reason to eliminate them.

To avoid hurting those owning modest amounts of intangible property—accumulated for retirement, children's educations, etc.—the federal government might copy Florida and exempt the first several hundreds of thousands of dollars (or, alternatively, exempt specifically accumulations of intangible property in pension funds or retirement accounts, etc.). Capable legislators could easily find and, with experience, refine the laws needed to tap the one major kind of property that has gone untaxed in most of this country for most of the last century.

During the last twenty years, the US experienced a rapid rise in the values of tangible property (especially real estate) and intangible property (especially stocks). For the many in our country who own their own homes, rising home values raised their property taxes. For the many who rent, the rising tangible property taxes paid by their landlords were passed on to them as higher rents. For the relatively few who own significant amounts of stocks and bonds—whose values skyrocketed—their increased intangible property holdings escaped all property taxes. How very nice for them. How costly for everyone else.

Consumerism: Curses and Causes

30 April 2008

US consumerism—citizens driven excessively to buy goods and services and accumulate consumable wealth—is cursed almost everywhere. Many environmentalists blame it for global warming. Critics of the current economic disasters often point to home-buying gluttony as the cause. Many see consumerism behind the borrowing that makes the US the world's greatest debtor nation today. Moralists of otherwise diverse motivations agree on attacking consumerist materialism as against spiritual values. Educators blame it for distracting young people's interest from learning. Psychologists attribute mass loneliness and depression to unrealizable expectations of what commodities can deliver to consumers. Physicians decry the diseases, stress, and exhaustion linked to excessive work driven by desire for excessive consumption. Yet, for a long time, exhortations by all such folks have mostly failed to slow, let alone reverse, US consumerism.

The question is why? The answer is not advertising, since that begs the question of why that industry should have been so successful in the US and grown to such influence. Nor is it plausible to attribute some national personality flaw to our citizens.

A big part of the answer lies in the unique history of US capitalism. From 1820 to 1970, over every decade, average real wages rose, enabling a rising standard of consumption. These 150 years rooted workers' beliefs that the US was a "chosen" place where every generation would live better than its parents. This was "the good news" of US capitalism for the workers. The "bad news" was that the average worker's productivity—the amount of output each worker produced for his/her employer to sell—rose even faster. This was because workers were relentlessly driven by employers to work harder, faster, and with ever more (and more complicated) machinery. Thus, alongside rising workers' wages, faster rising productivity brought even bigger gains for employers.

An unspoken, historic deal defined US capitalism for those 150 years. Capitalists paid rising wages to enable rising working-class consumption; the workers had to provide rising work effort, rising profitability, and thus the even faster rise of profits. Because the rise in workers' consumption was slower than the rise of their productivity—the output that they delivered to employers—the gap between workers and employers widened across US history. A fundamentally unequal society emerged, one that forever mocked, challenged, and undermined the ideological claims of the US to be the land of equality and opportunity. The working class labored ever harder, consumed more, and yet fell ever further behind the minority who lived off the growing difference between what workers produced and their wages.

This deal might have collapsed at any time if US workers rebelled against the organization of production in the US. This could have occurred if rising wages did not suffice to make them ignore the growing inequality of US life, or if they rejected subordination to ever more automated, exhausting work disciplines, or if they refused to deliver ever more wealth to ever fewer corporate boards of directors of immense corporations ever further removed from them in power, wealth, and access to culture. For that deal to survive—for US capitalism to have been "successful" for so long—something had to emerge in US society that prevented any of these deal-breakers from happening. Enter consumerism!

The idea settled into US culture that consumption was the proper goal of work and the measure of personal worth, of one's "success" in life. Business boosters and ideologues pushed that idea, but they were hardly alone. Advertisers made it their constant message. Trade unions focused also on raising wages and consumption—just what US capitalism could and did deliver—rather than challenging the organization of production. So too did most left movements. Economists did their part by building modern economics on the unquestioned axiom that labor was a burden for which consumption enabled by wages was the compensation. This definition of economics required banishing the alternative of Marxian economics from schools. The mass media proceeded as if it were likewise obvious common sense that all any employee *really* cared about was the size of his/her wage/salary. Of course, some dissident voices—especially on the left—rejected these ideas and this capital/labor deal, but consumerism usually all but drowned them out.

Consumerism's deep roots in the psyche of US workers explains their reactions when real wages stopped rising in the 1970s and since. They simply kept on buying more commodities. To pay for them, workers took on more hours of labor and borrowed vast sums. Worker exhaustion rose accordingly, likewise the number of family members sent out to work (straining "family values" to the breaking point). Anxiety intensified over frightening family debt levels. In this situation, the current scandal of sub-prime mortgages was a predictable disaster waiting to happen.

The 150-year deal has been broken. The business side no longer needs it; it hasn't since the 1970s. That is why real wages stopped rising. Most workers just postponed facing that reality and its implications: by having more family members do more work and by heavy borrowing. Meanwhile, able and willing laborers abroad who accept wages far lower than in the US beckon. US corporations are moving to produce there. They will ship "home" the goods and services they produce abroad so long as US citizens can afford them. When that no longer pays, they will redirect shipments to the rest of the world market.

Consumerism was a necessary component of US capitalism from the 1820s to the 1970s. As an ideology uniquely suited to that capitalism, it was articulated, cultivated, and supported by different social groups. Whatever fun comedians and critics poke at consumerism, it was not some lovable human foible, nor some quirk of our culture. It was the glue holding US capitalism together for a long time. Even more important, business dissolved that glue in the 1970s, and now US workers have exhausted ways to postpone the results of that dissolution. Storms are rising.

Nominating Palin Makes Sense

13 September 2008

If something is better than nothing, then Palin's nomination gives Americans just that choice and so another chance for the Republicans.

For the last 30 years, Republicans systematically aided capital in keeping real wages flat while raising productivity. That combination yielded exploding profits and exploding incomes for those who got their hands on those profits. The Republicans actively altered government taxing and spending patterns to further boost corporate profits while squeezing the workers (via reduced state services and jobs, etc.). The Democratic Party could or would not stop this process, often supported it, and only sometimes slowed it.

In the absence of any significant political party or movement of the working classes, the results of these 30 years include: (1) US workers responded to flat wages per hour by sending more family workers into the paid labor force and averaging *20 percent more labor hours per year* than they did in 1975, (2) working families borrowed vast sums to land more deeply in debt than ever before in US history, (3) work exhaustion and debt anxiety produced extreme levels of stress reflected in divorce, family breakdown, loneliness, legal and illegal drug dependencies, etc. Dissolving American families also confront the ever-wider divide between themselves and the rich top tenth. Wal-mart and Costco welcome (but also humiliate) families falling ever further behind the levels of consumption that define success and self-worth in our culture.

The Republicans long ago grasped their political vulnerability to being blamed for facilitating this state of affairs. To avoid that blame—and the resulting electoral losses—they spent their money to craft the image of Republicans as champions of a return to the "good old days" of US working families. Then, "family values" prevailed: married couples stayed together; they had the time and space to raise nice children, go proudly to church, cheer our troops as they spread freedom, and do fun leisure activities together. Then, they could afford "the suburban middle-class lifestyle" and so on. *A vote for the Republicans would somehow bring us all back to those times; at least the Republicans would try to do that.*

The Democrats split. One part, seeing the power of the Republicans' image, wanted to mimic it. They never figured out how to do that without appearing to be a poor, less believable copy. The other part of the Democratic Party saw through the crude Republican manipulation, scoffed at their image as phony and pandering, and tried instead to expose the Republicans' complicity in the workers' problems, to blame them in politically advantageous ways. This part—the more "liberal" or even "leftist" Democrats—could never go very far along these lines because the Democratic Party also needed the money and support of capital to pay the huge costs of political campaigns. The Democratic Party fears that alienating capital would assure Republican victories. So the Democratic Party usually presents policies and politicians that try to keep its two parts from breaking apart (since that would also, they fear, assure Republican dominance).

Therefore, the Democratic Party has basically offered the mass of US workers nothing real or concrete to *significantly* change their deteriorating social and personal situations. At best, Democratic Party rhetoric empathizes with their problems and more or less believably commits to improve things a bit. But nothing is likely from the Democrats that could *alter the basic components of the workers' deepening crises*—their wage and job prospects, the extent of state programs and supports they can obtain, their collapsing families and personal relationships, their dwindling self-confidence and frightening loneliness.

The problem for the Republicans in 2008 was that Bush had stretched popular credulity in their carefully crafted images to the breaking point. The Republican Party had not returned America to those good old days, which seemed further away than ever. Workers wanted change even if championed by an African-American who offered no more than another standard—and well-worded—version of the kind of Democratic Party position that tries to keep its two parts together. Nor could McCain plausibly represent, let alone renew and revive, the Republicans' self-presentation as a champion of hometown family values.

Hence the Palin choice. One more Republican shot at repeating what worked so well, but now needs to be done more aggressively than before because Bush and Cheney wore the image thin. Palin, as packaged, is the concretized fantasy of "hometown family values" carefully combined with personal flaws to be identified with, enthusiastic patriotism, aggressive celebration of capital's agenda, and status as maligned victim of elite and media hostility. By naming her, the Republicans aim yet again and more dramatically to be seen as the best hope American working people have that something, rather than nothing, may possibly be done for them in this time of looming economic catastrophe. Even something that is a long shot and a rerun of a fantasy not realized before is better than nothing. Hope, however far-fetched, is often chosen over resignation.

PART II: ECONOMICS OF THE CRISIS

The global crisis erupted first and foremost in the US economy. From there, its consequences radiate out to impose mounting costs on the rest of society and across the world. The essays in Part II focus on economics: how and why the production and distribution of goods and services broke down. The current economic crisis is compared to others. Some essays explore the relationships of key economic institutions—markets, the oil and housing industries, finance and real estate, pensions, household debt, and others—to the generation or spread of the crisis across the economy. The US economy's contributions and connections to crises in other countries—for example the UK, China, and Mexico—are considered. Other essays examine the economic policies of the US government and especially the Federal Reserve; here the basic question of what policy can do is introduced, while that question is further considered in Part III's essays.

Several essays in Part II discuss how economic theory has both shaped and been shaped by capitalist economic crises. Politicians, mass media managers, and academics act in part according to what they believe about how economies work. Because their actions contributed to producing and spreading the crisis, the economic theories they believed mattered. Any serious analysis of the economics of the crisis must include some attention to the influential or "mainstream" economic theories. It is also necessary to consider those economic theories that construct a critical analysis of the capitalist system (partly in response to its crises). By far the most important and developed of such critical theories are those originated by Marx and later Marxists. The insights of one such Marxist critical theory are also explored in this Part's essays.

Within each part and chapter of this book, the essays are presented in the order of the dates of their publication. Particularly throughout Part II, it may be useful to readers to follow this order as a kind of economic diary of an unfolding crisis. The essays progress from seeing the signs of danger into monitoring an intensifying crisis. Then they shift as the crisis erupts, spreads, and resists containment.

1. Capitalism as a Crisis-Prone System

Capitalism's Three Oscillations and the US Today

27 March 2007

Throughout its history and across its geography, capitalism has swung back and forth between private and state forms. The former reduces while the latter enlarges the state's intervention in the economy. The economic events that precipitate swings (in both directions) have been various mixes of recession and widening inequality. Political oscillations have paralleled the economic. Often the party or faction losing power is the one most closely associated with the kind of capitalism being displaced, while the ascendant party or faction champions the other kind. Cultural oscillations complete the interconnected tableau. For example, in the economic theorizing of the politicians, professors, and journalists, celebrations of private capitalism (variously named liberalism, neoliberalism, neoclassical economics, microeconomics, and so on) oscillate with celebrations of state capitalism (variously named welfare statism, Keynesianism, central planning, macroeconomics, and so on).

Abundant evidence suggests that these three sorts of oscillations—economic, political, and cultural—function simultaneously as causes and effects of one another. Together they comprise a web that serves sometimes to contain the contradictions of the system as a whole. In that sense, capitalism survives because it can resolve the crises of one kind of capitalism by a transition to the other kind rather than a transition out of capitalism. Yet the web of interdependence among its economic, political, and cultural oscillations may alternatively magnify a crisis of one kind of capitalism into a social demand for transition out of capitalism.

In the US, a crisis of private capitalism in the late 1920s was associated with oscillations to state capitalism, to welfare state economics, and to the Democratic Party. In the late 1970s, the reverse swings occurred. The web of interdependence among economics, politics, and culture worked in these instances to contain the contradictions of capitalism. That web enabled the crafting of a New Deal in the 1930s to preserve the basic system from dissolution and transition to another system. Later, in the 1960s and 1970s, that web precluded disaffection with the post-war US welfare state from producing a transition beyond capitalism and instead accomplished a relatively popular shift back to private capitalism. Perhaps, as others have argued, no system disappears until it has exhausted all its possible forms and oscillations.

For this argument to make sense, we need first and foremost to define carefully what we mean by the capitalist system. Borrowing from Marx's careful analysis, "capitalism" refers to the system of production in which a relatively large group of people (productive laborers) sell their capacity to work to a relatively small group of different people (capitalist employers) for an agreed payment. The capitalist employers provide the "means of production" (tools, equipment, and raw material) for the productive laborers to work with and on. There are two key aspects of the relationship between capitalists and productive laborers. First, what the laborers produce belongs instantly and automatically to the capitalist who sells it. Second, the revenue from that sale must exceed what the capitalist paid for the means of production and to the productive laborers. The excess is the surplus, the fund from which the capitalist distributes portions to reproduce capitalism as a system (portions including interest to creditors, dividends to shareholders, budgets to managers and advertisers, profits retained for enterprise growth, etc.).

In the private kind of capitalism, the employers have no position within a state apparatus. Moreover, the state's functionaries exercise quite limited powers over the relationships among and between employers and laborers. By contrast, in the state kind of capitalism, state functionaries have much greater powers to regulate, control, and intervene in the relationships among and between employers and employees. Extreme state capitalism finds state functionaries replacing private individuals as capitalist employers (in "state-owned" enterprises) and thereby directly appropriating and distributing the surpluses produced by productive laborers. What both kinds of capitalism have in common—what makes them alternative kinds of one system—is the shared structure of the surplus-yielding employer/employee relationship.

A social crisis of either kind of capitalism could go beyond merely a transition to the other kind. It could entail a basic change in the capitalist relationship between employer and employee. One example of such a basic change would be a social reorganization of production requiring employers and productive employees to be the same individuals. Job descriptions would then mandate that productive laborers work Mondays through Thursdays on making output, while on Fridays they would assemble to function collectively as their own board of directors.

Is the US now entering another crisis-cum-transition period? Thirty-five years of rolling back the New Deal did return and renew private capitalism. Republicans displaced Democrats (and among Democrats, the anti-welfare statist faction replaced the pro-welfare statist one). Neoclassical and neoliberal economic theories vanquished Keynesian economics in the schools and refashioned "common sense" about economic issues. Yet US private capitalism since early 2000 has suffered a stock market bubble's burst whose effects are still ramifying. Now a real estate bubble totters with troubling consequences. Worries grow about international financial markets—increasingly mysterious in their multiplying layers of new instruments and increasingly opaque. Will finance be yet a third bubble of the new millennium? Can the private kind of capitalism survive all this?

Widening income and wealth disparities associated with private capitalism's resurgence helped already to provoke a US political oscillation. The Republican coalition (advocates of private capitalism allied with religious fundamentalism) cracked partly because of those disparities. By adding to and fueling opposition to the Iraq war, growing social inequalities switched Congress to the Democrats in 2006. (Similarly, the unequal benefits from state-interventionist capitalism had undermined the Democratic party's coalition in the 1970s and thereby enabled Reagan's victories in the 1980s.) Elsewhere today, especially in Latin America, neoliberalisms in economic theory and in politics are shifting back toward welfare statism. These winds of change raise two interconnected questions yet again. First, will the still dominant private capitalism be able to keep its current US crisis under control? Second, if not, will transition be limited again to welfare statism in economics, Keynesianism in theory, and Democrats in politics? Or might today's conditions persuade enough Americans that a more basic transition—out of capitalism—is the needed solution?

This last transition will not likely occur without a strong social movement for it. Is that not a major task for a resurgent left in the US?

Financial Panics, Then and Now

21 August 2007

The authors of the most widely read book on financial panics (*Manias, Panics, and Crashes: A History of Financial Crises*, Fifth Edition, 2005) refer to them as "hardy perennials" and document how they have repeatedly devastated large portions of modern economies and societies over the last three centuries. Charles Kindleberger (professor of economics at MIT until his death in 2003) and Robert Aliber (professor of economics and finance at the University of Chicago; he is responsible for this latest edition) also write that the period since the 1970s has been the most economically tumultuous in all that time. The last few weeks certainly reinforce that judgment.

The ingredients of financial panics are boringly repetitive. Past panics fade from memory. Financial institutions figure out ways to circumvent the regulations established to prevent those past panics from happening again. Rising asset prices enable easier credit and vice versa. Market euphoria grips increasing numbers. Risks are underestimated. Quick, large fortunes are made and flaunted. Everyone seeks to ride the economic boom times to great wealth. All the conditions are in place for something significant to go wrong. Sometimes it is a sudden demonstration that risks were greater than understood or admitted. Today that is what has happened to sub-prime mortgages and the mortgage-backed securities dependent on them. Sometimes it is a crisis of the lenders who can no longer extend easy credit to borrowers dependent on it. Today that includes hedge funds experiencing depletion of the funds entrusted to them by investors frightened by the prospects of the financial and economic meltdowns that often follow panics. Sometimes it is a crisis of the borrowers who simply cannot maintain the growth of indebtedness upon which the market euphoria depends. Today that is what is happening as businesses and consumers face levels of debt repayment, declining home prices, and rising energy costs that combine to make them less willing to borrow and spend as they had for the last quarter century. One or more of the things that can go wrong eventually do and then the sweet economy can turn sour fast.

As has happened so many times before, the ride up the economic boom is as thrilling as the crash down is depressing. Likewise, the boastful assertions during the boom about government economic intervention being unnecessary and counterproductive give way to desperate cries for government bailouts (acting as "lender of last resort" when the private credit markets have stopped functioning). The Fed is now acting out this old scenario yet again. Millions bemoan the trillions in value vanishing in these uniquely capitalist orgies of self-destruction. Experts in the US real estate markets now estimate that 2 million families will lose their new homes by the end of 2008 or early 2009. For these 8–10 million citizens and the countless friends, relatives, businesses, and communities that depend on them—extreme economic hardships loom. Bankruptcies, unemployment, delayed or cancelled visits to doctors, reduced enrollments and rising absences in schools, postponed home and auto repairs, and so on will cause incalculable economic and social losses for years into the future. So too will the extra strains on and obstacles for interpersonal relationships among adults and between them and children.

Of course, capitalism's defenders and champions are ready to disseminate explanations that put these disasters in better light. We will be told that the workers and businesses collapsing around us were the "inefficient" ones and that their elimination serves to make the economy as a whole healthier and more successful. This metaphorical use of Darwin's theory of natural selection will coexist with creationism as parallel modes of rejecting unwelcome alternative explanations. The blame for economic disaster will be heaped on government regulations, taxes, and programs that prevented the wonderful things private enterprise would otherwise surely have done. Other scapegoats attacked these days—to explain the economic disasters or at least distract attention from them—include "terrorists," immigrants, outsourcing, China, and so on.

Meanwhile, the wreckage will ramify. Millions of families will alter their lives to accommodate lost homes, jobs, educations, and relationships. Resources will rust and rot from disuse. It will take time—and the associated suffering—for wages to fall far enough to make profit rates high enough to lure capital back in. The painful wait for that will revive the hoary old debate in the US between conservatives and liberals. The former will insist that the private market is best left to its own devices to end the downturn and return to better economic times. The liberals will demand a more or less welfare-state type of government intervention to provide jobs, incomes, healthcare, subsidized housing, and so on. Whichever side "wins," the other side will set to work to undo the victory. Sooner or later, the winning side will encounter yet another financial panic that produces enough pain and suffering to allow the side that lost before to win now by promising to fix the broken economy. Then the whole sorry story gets replayed yet again.

The Great Depression of 1929 yielded such a victory to FDR's New Deal and its Keynesian economics. The Republicans went to work to undo FDR and his legacy, while Milton Friedman and his ilk went to work to undo Keynesian economics. Neither succeeded until the US economy experienced a meltdown in the 1970s. Recall a few facts. In the middle of the decade the US experienced the worst recession since the Great Depression. Gold at the beginning of that decade cost $40 per ounce; by the end it cost $1,000 per ounce. Petroleum went from $2.50 per barrel to $40. The US dollar lost more than half its value relative to the German mark and the Japanese yen across the 1970s. Perhaps most relevant to the here and now is this statistic: during the 1970s, the real rate of return on holding stocks and bonds (that is the return adjusted for price inflation) was negative. By contrast, in the 1990s, the real rate of return on stocks and bonds averaged 15 percent per year. Severe economic problems throughout the 1970s strengthened the

Republicans sufficiently to allow them to undo and reverse the New Deal: Reagan's "revolution."

With the next panic, set off by the US stock market's burst bubble early in 2000, the debate revived. Paul Krugman and his ilk could then revive the "state intervention is necessary" song and dance. George Bush could fight a losing battle to stave off the collapse and undoing of the Reagan revolution he had hoped to complete. Millions of Americans (and millions more abroad) are today poised to bear the costs of yet another financial panic, the one unfolding now. Perhaps it will yield another oscillation between the private market and the state-interventionist forms of capitalism. This pattern will continue unless and until the old question is asked again, the question about alternatives to both forms, and a new answer given.

Neoliberal Globalization Is Not the Problem

4 December 2007

Capitalism is. The leftists who target neoliberal globalization denounce privatization, free markets, unfettered mobility of capital, and government deregulations of industry. They propose instead that national or supra-national governments control and regulate market transactions and especially capital movements, increase taxes on profits and wealth, and even own and operate industry. "All in the interests of the people," they say, democratically.

Yet Marx's critique of capitalism never focused on government regulations, interventions, and state-owned industries. They were never his solutions for the costs, injustices, and wastes of capitalism. Instead, Marx targeted and stressed capitalism's "class structure" of production. By this he meant how productive enterprises were internally organized: tiny groups of people (boards of directors) who appropriated a portion—the "surplus"—from what the laborers produced and the enterprise sold. Marx defined such surplus appropriation as "exploitation." *And, as Marx said, capitalist exploitation can exist whether those appropriators are corporate boards of directors (private capitalism) or state officials (state capitalism).*

Marx opposed capitalism's exploitative class structure of production on political, ethical, and economic grounds. He preferred a communist alternative where productive workers functioned as their own board of directors, collectively appropriating and distributing the surpluses they produced. Equality and democracy, he argued, required the abolition of exploitation as a necessary condition of their realization.

Capitalism as a system has always and everywhere gone through phases, repeated swings between two alternative forms. Private capitalism is the neoliberal, "laissez-faire" form: government intervention in economic affairs is minimized, and individuals and businesses interact largely through voluntary market exchanges. The other form is state-interventionist, "social democratic," welfare-state capitalism: government manages the economy by regulating what the private capitalists can do or by sometimes even taking over their enterprises to turn business decisions into government decisions.

Every few decades, in every capitalist country, whichever of these two forms has been in place runs into serious economic difficulty. Workers lose jobs, incomes decline, enterprises fail, and so on. The cry arises that "something must be done." Those feeling the least pain and making good money prefer to let the existing form of capitalism correct itself. Those hurting the most and losing money demand more drastic change. When this second group prevails politically, the existing form of capitalism is ended and the other installed. A few decades later the same drama is played out in reverse.

When a booming private capitalism in the US hit a stone wall in 1929, the country shifted over into welfare-state capitalism. When the 1960s and 1970s produced crises in that welfare-state capitalism, the country shifted over to private capitalism (neoliberalism). Now, after thirty years of globalized private capitalism yield proliferating difficulties, too many leftists have joined the chorus that sees the only solution in yet another swing back to welfare-state capitalism. The legacy of Coolidge and Hoover was overthrown by FDR's chorus. The legacy of the New Deal was overthrown by Ronald Reagan's chorus. The Reagan-Bush legacy may now be overthrown by Clinton, Obama, et al. Such phased reversals between capitalism's two forms occur nearly everywhere, varying only with each country's particular conditions and history.

As forms, private and state capitalism are oscillating phases of the capitalist system. When one phase cannot solve its problems, the solution has been a shift to the other phase. Thus, crises of capitalism have so far avoided provoking the alternative solution of a transition out of capitalism. Yet that transition was precisely Marx's goal. He aimed to persuade workers that oscillations between state and private capitalism were not the best solutions to capitalism's failings, at least not for workers.

Many leftists today catalog the awful results of 25 years of neoliberal dominance: economic and social crises punctuating ever deeper inequalities of wealth, income, and power across and within most nations. They cite the burst investment bubbles, unsustainable debt explosions, collapsed credit markets, threats of recession, crumbling social services, unsafe commodity production, and so forth. They propose "solutions": governments—national or maybe now supranational—must be recalled by a democratic upsurge to their proper role. Governments should limit, control, regulate, or replace private capitalist enterprises in the interests of the people.

This way of thinking repeats the left's mistakes in the 1930s. Then, when private capitalism had imploded into the Great Depression, deteriorating conditions turned most Americans against the likes of Republican Herbert Hoover and toward Democratic FDR. A new era of government economic intervention took the name Keynesian economics. However, New Deal Keynesianism always left in place the private boards of directors of the capitalist corporations that dominated the US economy. Those boards remained as the receivers of the surplus produced by their workers—the corporations' "profits." They used those profits to grow the corporations, to make still more profits, to pay higher salaries to top officers, to influence politics, and so on.

Welfare-state capitalism in the US imposed taxes, regulations, and limits on—and mass employment alternatives to—those private corporations. But by leaving their boards of directors in place as the receivers and dispensers of corporate profits, the welfare state *signed its own death warrant*. The boards of directors had the desire and the means to undo the welfare state. It took them a while to change public opinion and build a rich and powerful movement led by business to achieve their goals. In the Reagan administration and since, enabled by a crisis of the welfare state in the 1960s and 1970s, they succeeded in switching the US and beyond back to a phase of private capitalism we call "neoliberal globalization."

Understandably, many people cannot see beyond capitalism's two phases or the debates, struggles, and transitions between them. But leftists who see no further—who criticize neoliberal globalization and advocate a warmed-over welfare-state Keynesianism—have abandoned Marx's critical *anti-capitalist* project. They have become just another chorus for yet another oscillation back to the welfare state form of capitalism.

The working classes need and deserve better than that, now more than ever.

Economic Blues

7 July 2008

Housing and securities prices are going down; food and fuel prices are rising. How will these opposite trends affect our economy looking ahead?

The real estate bubble (US capitalism's latest toxic mix of profit-driven over-investment, over-lending, and financial fraud) is in full "bust" mode. Residential and now also commercial real estate prices are dropping quickly. Millions of families who used their rising home prices over the last decade to borrow money (the "refinancing" boom) can no longer do so. Their consumption thereupon falls as do the fortunes of all the producers who depend on that consumption. As other home "owners" default by the millions on unsustainable mortgages, foreclosures throw ever more houses onto a market with many fewer buyers. This drives home prices down further and likewise consumption. This process is now leading world capitalism into a global slowdown in production.

At the same time, the world of financial investing (banks, hedge funds, stockbrokers, etc.) is reeling from widening real estate losses. Investors globally bought billions of US securities based on US mortgages (and other kinds of loans) whose borrowers cannot make the required repayments. First these big investors produced the real estate bubble monster and now they scramble to survive its bursting, to avoid fates like that of Bear Stearns. So they cut back credit to still other borrowers who now struggle to cope with lost borrowing capability. This too contributes to the global slowdown. Modern capitalism is caught up in yet another Frankenstein story.

Large investors are changing their portfolios. They are not returning massively into stocks, remembering their losses in 2000 when the dot-com bubble burst in another Frankenstein horror. The global slowdown likewise undercuts stock buying. Nor will they soon return to the downward spiraling real estate market. So they are looking for new places to put their money.

The big investors are also worried about the risks of inflation. They know that the US government pumped historically unprecedented mountains of new money into the world economy in its "policies" to offset and cushion the social effects of first the stock market meltdown of 2000 and then the real estate bubble bursting since 2006. They fear that all this extra money in circulation may well be used, sooner or later, to make purchases and thereby bid up prices. Fearing such inflation, they don't hold money as an asset (a form of their wealth) because money's value—its purchasing power—drops when commodity prices rise.

Instead, they buy commodities whose prices they think will rise fastest: not to consume or use them, but rather to hold and resell them later at the higher prices. These days, those commodities include energy, food, basic production materials (metals, minerals, etc.), and gold and silver. Many factors (difficulties in finding new sources of these things, climate changes, rising production in newly industrializing countries, etc.) combine to make their prices rise the fastest. So big investors buy them and contribute further to the inflation from which they seek to profit. Media and politicians' eagerness to blame "speculators"—bad people are the problem—divert attention from how global capitalism repeatedly provokes investment bubbles and then spreads the damage when they burst, including the damage from inflation.

The system is the problem. US capitalism is dysfunctional on many levels for working people today. It is driving down the value of their most important asset, their homes; it is reducing the credit that their standard of living now depends on; it is slowing production, which drives up unemployment; and it is driving up the prices of the food and fuel they cannot do without. This is what capitalism delivers these days.

Because profit-driven agricultural corporations displaced family farming, our food supply became much more energy-dependent (for tractors, fertilizer, insecticides, and for transporting food products). So rising energy prices provoke rising food prices. The drive of US business to profit from suburbanization vastly increased Americans' dependence on energy (for cars, electricity, and heating single-family homes). So rising energy prices raise the cost of living especially in the suburbs, where most Americans live.

Of course, a government responsible to its people and aware of US capitalism's history could have anticipated and taken some steps at least to reduce the damage from the latest bouts of booms, busts, speculations, and inflations. However, the last 30 years of Republican and Democratic governments did none of that. They celebrated "private enterprise" and *less* government economic intervention. So, for example, local non-energy-guzzling farming was not encouraged, subsidized, studied, or even officially discussed as an agricultural policy. Nor was substituting energy-saving mass transit for the individual automobile, nor cheaper housing options than energy-guzzling single-family homes. Instead, corporations profited from making us increasingly dependent on energy—despite available alternatives—and threatened by its rising price.

To answer the question we began with: there is no way now to tell how falling real estate and securities markets will interact with rising food and energy and materials prices in terms of their impacts on overall inflation, production, employment, and incomes. No one knows, including those private and government "experts" and "officials" who pretend, like the fortunetellers at the county fair, that they see into the future.

But American working people should face certain facts about the economic system they live with. So long as private corporations wield the power to use the profits they get from selling the products their workers produce, they will continue to do what they have always done. They will deploy those profits to competitively seek higher profits, produce booms and busts, speculations, speculators, and inflations. And they will use those profits to buy the politicians and the media to make sure they and the system that funds them receive no blame for any of it. The system is the problem.

Capitalist Crisis, Marx's Shadow

26 September 2008

Capitalism happens. When and where it does, capitalism casts its own special shadow: a self-critique of capitalism's basic flaws that says modern society can do better by establishing very different, post-capitalist economic systems. This critical shadow rises up to terrify capitalism when—in crisis periods such as now—capitalism hits the fan. Karl Marx poetically called that shadow the specter that haunts capitalism.

The so-called *financial* crisis today is a symptom. The underlying disease is capitalism: an economic system that weaves implacable and destructive conflict into its production and distribution of goods and services. Employers and employees need to cooperate to make the economy work, but they are forever adversaries whose conflicts periodically burst into crises. So it is today. Capitalism also locks employers into those endless struggles with and against one another that we call competition. It too periodically erupts into conflicts and crises. And so it is today.

Employer-employee conflict contributed to today's global capitalist meltdown as follows. In the 1970s, employers found a way to stop the long-term slow rise in real wages of their employees. By outsourcing jobs overseas to take advantage of cheaper wages, by drawing US women into the labor force, by substituting computers and other machines for workers, and by bringing in low-wage immigrants, employers drove down their employees' wages even as they produced ever more commodities for sale. The results were predictable. On the one hand, company profits soared (after all, workers produced ever more while not having to be paid more). One the other hand, after a few years, stagnant workers' wages proved insufficient to enable them to buy the growing output of their labor. Given how capitalism works, employers unable to sell all that they produce lay off their own employees. And of course, that only compounds the problem.

Thus, in the 1970s, another capitalist crisis loomed as a bad recession hit hard. But that crisis was kept short because US capitalism found a way to postpone it: massive debt. Since employers succeeded in keeping wages from rising, the only way to sell the ever-expanding output was to *lend* workers the money to buy more. Corporations invested their soaring profits in buying new securities backed by workers' mortgages, auto loans, and credit-card loans. Owners of such securities were thereby entitled to portions of the monthly payments workers made on those loans. In effect, the extra profits made by keeping workers' wages down now did double duty for employers who earned hefty interest payments by loaning part of those profits back to the workers. What a system!

Postponing the solution to the crisis of the 1970s only prepared the way for the bigger one now. Booming consumer lending in the 1980s, 1990s, and since 2000, especially in the deregulated financial world of Reagan and Bush America, provoked wild profit-driven excesses and corruption (the stock market "bubble" and then the real estate "bubble"). It also loaded millions of Americans with unsustainable debts. By 2006, the most stressed borrowers—"sub-prime"—could no longer pay what they owed. This house of debt cards then began its spiraling descent.

Competition among enterprises also contributed to this crisis. As some banks made big profits rushing to lend to workers, other lenders feared that those banks would use those profits to outcompete them. So they too rushed into "consumer lending." To raise the money to make such profitable loans to workers, lenders made expanded use of new types of financial instruments, chiefly securities backed by workers' debt obligations (securities whose owners received portions of workers' loan repayments). US lenders sold these securities globally to tap into the entire world's cash. The whole world thus got drawn into depending on a whirlpool: US capitalism propping up its workers' purchasing power with costly loans because it no longer raised their wages. The competing rating companies

(Fitch, Moody's, Standard and Poor, etc.) inaccurately assessed these securities' riskiness. These companies competed for the business of lenders who needed high ratings to sell the debt-backed securities. Private and public lenders around the world competed with one another by buying the US debt-backed securities because they were rated as nearly riskless and yet paid high interest rates.

Enterprise competition and employer-employee conflicts—both core components of capitalism—have been major causes of today's "financial crisis." Yet the huge government bailout now proposed by Treasury Secretary Paulson and Fed Chairman Bernanke does not address either the problem of stagnant wages or that of competition. Instead the proposed bailout plans to "fix" the financial crisis by throwing vast sums at the big lenders in the *hope* that they will resume lending and so pull the economy out of its crisis. Because this "solution" ignores the underlying problems of our capitalist economy, its prospects for success are poor.

No questioning, let alone challenging, of capitalism's role is conceivable for US leaders. Quite the contrary, their "policies" aim chiefly to preserve capitalism—largely by keeping its responsibility for the current crisis out of public debate and thus away from political action. Yet this crisis, like many others, raises Marx's specter, capitalism's shadow, once again. The specter's two basic messages are clear: (1) today's global financial crisis flows from core components of the capitalist system and (2) to really solve the current crisis requires changing those components to move society beyond capitalism.

For example, if workers in each enterprise became their own collective boards of directors, the old capitalist conflicts between employers and employees would be overcome. If state agencies coordinated enterprises' interdependent production decisions, the remaining enterprise competition could be limited to focus on rewards for improved performance. The US government might not just bail out huge financial institutions but also require them to change into enterprises where employers and employees were the same people and where coordination and competition became the major and minor aspects of enterprise interactions. The US government took over Fannie Mae, Freddie Mac, and AIG, but it changed neither the organization of these enterprises nor the destructive competition among them. That was a tragically lost opportunity. If the political winds continue to change far enough and fast enough, solutions responding to the current crisis by moving beyond capitalism might yet be tried.

Wall Street vs. Main Street: Finger Pointing vs. System Change

14 October 2008

Amid the current capitalist crisis, fear spreads and scapegoating surges. Media and politicians charge the predictable suspects. Arrests may follow. Few recognize the system as the problem, rather than this or that group reacting to the system's demands and pressures. True, the word "capitalism" now arises in public discussion. But there it means big business, big banks, or Wall Street, rather than the system that ties together all streets, businesses, workers, households, and the government.

Cruder right-wingers scapegoat the homebuyers now unable to pay for their sub-prime mortgages. The slightly more sophisticated denounce government intervention—to help minorities and the poor become homeowners—for whatever ails the economy. The crudest of all blend Wall Street, bankers, and crooked Washington insiders into conspiracies to profit personally and/or sell out the US to world communism or terrorism or maybe Muslims.

On the left, favorite whipping boys include Wall Street, bankers, hedge funds, overpaid executives, crooked corporations, and compromised politicians who let bad things happen "to our economy." More sophisticated leftists accelerate condemnations of "neoliberal deregulation." Ever since Reagan's election, they say, government failures to regulate markets and control private enterprises facilitated the wild financial misdeeds that have now brought us low.

Neither side treats the capitalist system as the basic problem. Rather, both mostly agree that the interacting network of corporations with their boards of directors, salaried managers, and wage workers are the necessary and appropriate foundations "of our economy." As that network, capitalism strikes them as inevitable, and thus *not* the appropriate target for right or left. Instead, they debate how much blame should attach to this or that group for "causing" the crisis: poor people or too much government intervention or too little or the overpaid rich with hedge funds or the corrupt bad apples fouling the system. Fingers point to culprits spoiling a capitalism—"our economy"—that would otherwise work just fine.

Consider the Wall Street vs. Main Street debate. Many leftists and not a few rightists accuse Wall Street of "causing" the sub-prime mortgage mess (as if countless Main Street banks and mortgage brokers had not pushed profitable mortgages onto locals unable to afford them). They scowl that Wall Street invented "derivatives," those dangerous new financial gimmicks (as if Main Street types did not invest in and profit from them). Leftists claim that Wall Street got politicians to deregulate the economy (as if many Main Street businesses did not likewise support and profit from deregulation). Many rightists claim that *insufficient* government deregulation, because of Wall Street influence, caused the crisis (as if Main Street did not benefit from that government intervention). Rightists and leftists both largely blame Wall Street and Washington for together producing the housing and real estate bubble (as if Main Street did not cheer the rising prices and building of houses, the booming demand for household products, the resulting jobs, incomes, and tax revenues, etc.).

As capitalism's latest boom goes bust, Wall Street and Main Street shift from mutually profitable cooperation to a struggle over survival. Main Street fears Wall Street will use its power, money, and influence to dump the pains of economic crisis onto workers and governments (by cutting wages and jobs, paying fewer taxes, and demanding more government aid and bailouts). This will hurt Main Street. Capitalism works to shift economic costs down the economic structure and economic gains upward. So Main Street fights back with public opinion campaigns to blame Wall Street for the crisis. In this falling out among thieves, left and right mostly take sides rather than reject the system that spawned those thieves. The alternative position would be to demand system change.

System change does *not* mean what Paulson and Bernanke now plan: to buy shares of private US banks. In this partial "nationalization" of the banks, the US government will buy and hold bank shares and possibly place state officials on the banks' boards of directors. Private enterprises thereby become, partly and probably temporarily, public enterprises. This change is big for Bush, Paulson, and Bernanke because they always denounced public enterprises as socialism or communism.

But replacing *private* members of bank boards of directors (elected by and responsible to private shareholders) with *public* members (named by and responsible to state officials) does not basically change the system. The workers still work 9 to 5; they still follow the board's orders; and the goods, services, and profits they produce belong to the boards of directors to serve their interests. Those boards, whether private or public, still give the orders, sell the products, receive the revenues, and decide how to use the profits. The profound inequalities between workers and board of directors remain. The profound absence of democracy in the capitalist workplace remains. Both public and private boards of directors have historically sought to evade, weaken, or eliminate state controls and regulations limiting their freedom of action and their profitability (in the USSR as well as the US).

Capitalism has everywhere oscillated between private and public phases. Private capitalism minimized government interventions and mostly kept state officials off boards of directors. In capitalism's public phases, governments intervened and sometimes replaced private with public members of boards of directors. Crises of one phase often provoked transition to the other. The 1929 crisis of private US capitalism ushered in Roosevelt's New Deal state intervention (establishing Social Security, unemployment insurance, and other costly—to business—programs and regulations). The 1970s crisis of state-regulated capitalism returned the US to another private capitalist phase, the Reagan-Bush era, which undid most of the New Deal. What will follow today's crisis of private capitalism?

Will the pendulum swing back to state re-regulated capitalism? If so, the US business community will utilize decades of accumulated expertise in how to evade, then weaken, and finally eliminate state regulation. Re-regulation will thus likely be short-lived. Or might the alternative of system change become important?

System change would supplement re-regulation with a transformation inside enterprises. Suppose old boards of directors were replaced by new boards whose members understood and shared the goals of regulation rather than seeing regulation as limitations to be undermined. This might happen if the new boards comprised the collectivity of the workers themselves. Job descriptions of all workers would henceforth combine the particular labor of each with her or his full participation in the collective tasks of the board of directors.

In this way, workers-as-also-bosses could both shape economic regulations—alongside other workers running other enterprises—and then carry them out inside each enterprise. The conflict of interests between employers and employees would be transformed once these were no longer different and opposed groups. This would be real system change. Without this, boards of directors, private and/or public, will continue to function in the future as they have in the past. They will undermine regulations aimed to make the economy serve society, will continue to run their enterprises undemocratically, will maintain economic inequalities, and will continue to generate economic crises like the one imposed on us all today.

Capitalism's Crisis through a Marxian Lens

14 December 2008

In Marxian terms, the current crisis emerged from the workings of the capitalist class structure. Capitalism's history displays repeated booms and busts punctuated by bubbles. Capitalism's cycles range unpredictably from local, shallow, and short to global, deep, and long. To keep capitalism is to suffer its chronic instability. To deal effectively with capitalism's *recurring* crises requires changing to a non-capitalist class structure.

Since the mid-1970s, workers' average real wages stopped rising. This was partly because capitalists' computerization of production displaced workers. Capitalists also decided then to move more production to foreign countries for higher profits. Since employers thus needed fewer workers in the US, they could and did end the historic (1820–1970) rise of US wages.

However, workers' productivity kept rising (more machines, more pressure, and more skills). They produced ever more for their employers to sell, yet the employers paid them no more. The *surpluses* extracted (exploited) by capitalist employers—the excess of the value added by each laborer over the value paid to that laborer—rose. The last 30 years realized capitalists' wildest dreams. Yet, stagnant wages and booming surpluses also eventually plunged US capitalism into today's severe crisis.

Today's major capitalists—corporate boards of directors—received most of those fast-rising surpluses. How they distributed those surpluses shaped our history. One huge portion went for top executives' payouts. Another portion increased dividends to corporations' shareholders (who, after all, elect boards of directors). Still other portions financed the transfer of production abroad, enhanced computerization to reduce payrolls, and lobbying for favorable state actions (e.g., reducing corporate taxes and allowing more immigration to lower wages).

Corporations deposited mounting surpluses in banks. Banks grew and invented new financial instruments to profit further from those surpluses. New instruments included securities such as "collateralized debt obligations" (comprised of mortgage, credit card, corporate, and student-loan debt); "credit default swaps" (deals to insure such new securities); and other "derivatives" for trading the risks of fast multiplying new credit instruments among those with the surpluses to invest. Because the new instruments operated completely outside existing regulations in a "shadow credit system" ever bigger risks were undertaken for ever bigger profits. Specialized enterprises such as hedge funds arose to invest rising corporate surpluses and exploding executive incomes in the murky shadows of high finance. Huge profits were made over the last 20 years, but the resulting capitalist exuberance once again overreached its limits.

The financial profits depended on the rising surpluses that depended on the stagnant wages. Financial profits also depended on the flip side of stagnant wages, namely massive worker borrowing. Because rising consumption had become the measure of personal success in life, wage stagnation since the 1970s rendered most US workers extraordinarily vulnerable to new consumer credit offers. Enter the banks relentlessly pushing credit cards, home equity loans, student loans, and so on. Workers undertook a record-breaking debt binge. The banks packaged that debt into new securities (the now infamous MBSs and CDOs) and sold them to all those seeking investments for their pieces of the soaring surpluses.

In effect, US capitalism thereby substituted rising loans for rising wages to workers. It took from them twice: first, the surplus their labor produced; and second, the interest on the surpluses lent back to them. This double squeeze on workers was the foundation of the US boom from the 1970s to 2006.

Eventually, the rising costs of the double squeeze strangled the boom. Families' rising indebtedness meant that illnesses, job losses, and divorces now yielded the added tragedy of defaults on debts. Rising steadily and ominously across 2007, defaults on credit-card debt, auto loans, student loans, and mortgages took off in 2008. The new kinds of securities based on workers' debts began to lose value in the markets. Banks, hedge funds, and others holding those securities faced mounting losses. Corporations that insured those securities via credit default swaps, etc., could not pay when so many securities' values collapsed. Banks had used their depositors' money and borrowed still more to buy such securities. Banks' losses prevented repaying those loans or guaranteeing their depositors' money. Financial markets froze as borrowers and lenders stopped trusting one another and drastically reduced transactions. Bust followed bubble followed boom, once again.

US corporate boards of directors had taken three interconnected steps to produce that sequence. They froze workers' real wages, they extracted much more surplus from their rising productivity, and they distributed that rising surplus in ways that were cumulatively unsustainable. Irrational capitalist exuberance once again overreached its limits. The capitalist system of producing and distributing surpluses proved itself yet again fundamentally crisis-prone.

Had this capitalist system been replaced by another, say one in which the workers who produced the surpluses in each enterprise also functioned as the collective appropriator and distributor of those surpluses, US history since the 1970s would have differed greatly. Workers appropriating their own surplus would likely NOT have frozen their real wages (hence no exploding consumer debt). Workers who collectively appropriated their own surpluses would likely NOT have given immense new payouts to top managers. The distribution of personal income would thus NOT have become so unequal across the last thirty years. Workers appropriating their own surpluses would likely NOT have devoted huge portions of them to move their jobs overseas. And so on.

Of course, such a class structure would have its own contradictions and problems. It would interact with political institutions in ways different from how capitalist class structures do. Gender equality, environmental sustainability, and many other issues would still need attention, but they would not be aggravated, for instance, by the aforementioned double squeeze.

Thus the urgent questions are: Will responses to this latest capitalist crisis continue to ignore or deny the role of capitalism's class structure? Will the crisis consequences of allowing capitalist boards of directors to appropriate and distribute surpluses go unrecognized? If so, the personal, political, economic, and cultural losses inflicted by this latest capitalist crisis will fail to teach their key lesson: a genuine solution requires progress beyond the capitalist class structure.

It's the System, Stupid

31 December 2008

At the capitalist system's core lies its central conflict. On one side, corporate boards of directors pursue ever *more* surplus extracted from productive workers. On the other side, workers seek ever more wages and benefits and better working conditions that *reduce* the surplus available to employers. Perpetual class conflict results between capitalists and workers over the size of that surplus. The conflict's form varies from hidden to open and from mild to violent.

Boards of directors continually find ways to reduce wages. Yet they complain when consumers whose wages fall cannot then buy all the commodities that capitalists need to sell to them. Indeed, insufficient consumption often contributes to causing or worsening a recession. The contradiction here is one that many capitalists seem unable to see, let alone trace to the class structure of capitalist production and its resulting conflict. Workers continually seek to improve their incomes, benefits, and job conditions. Yet they confront employers who respond by outsourcing jobs to cheaper or more subservient workers or by eliminating jobs through automation, even at the cost of jeopardizing commodity sales to workers, leading to or worsening recessions. The contradiction here—workers who achieve gains risk losing their jobs—underlies another of capitalism's systemic conflicts. As discussed further below, were workers to become their own collective boards of directors, they would not likely reduce wages or outsource jobs. Workers appropriating their own surpluses would accompany automation with serious job retraining and transitional support to displaced workers— rarely done when capitalist boards of directors automate.

Conflict between corporate directors and productive workers helped to produce both the wage stagnation of the last 25 years and the resulting surplus bubble that swelled and then burst in 2008. Class conflict has always contributed to capitalism's systemic instability. Just since the Second World War ended in 1945, there have been 11 recessions (including the latest that began in December 2007) according to the National Bureau of Economic Research, the official recession monitor of the US. Capitalism's instability was a constant, even though national politics and culture changed repeatedly after 1945, as the Cold War flared and ebbed. Capitalism's class structure kept hammering its rhythm of boom and bust cycles into our lives.

Each recession since 1948 cost *millions* of lost jobs that hurt the workers involved, their families, neighbors, and communities (including their employers). Large portions of productive capacity (machines, equipment, offices, stores) were idled: output worth *billions* that might have been produced never was because of recession. Had that output been produced and used to alleviate social problems (poverty, homelessness, inadequate childcare, deteriorated infrastructure, etc.), we would be living in a very different country. Recessions always cut revenues for local, state, and federal governments, forcing reductions in public education, healthcare, and so on. Recurring instability mocks as well as invalidates all that noise about "capitalist efficiency."

It would be reasonable to identify, investigate, and publicly discuss every possible cause of such instability. The goals would be to offset, moderate, or eliminate its effects or, better yet, the instability itself. But a taboo blocks consideration of one such cause, namely capitalism's class structure. For the last half-century, analyses and policies debated by most business, political, academic, and even labor leaders avoided connecting economic instability to capitalism's class structure. Instead, many faulted politicians (blaming Democrats or Republicans), unions, or big business. Others focused on human weaknesses ("greed," "irresponsible" borrowing, etc.). Still others blamed inadequate state "regulation" of private business. With most analyses blind to class structure as a cause, *change* in the class structure of production rarely figured in proposed solutions for capitalist instability.

The policies actually debated are all variations of (1) US state responses to the 1930s Great Depression and (2) Japanese state interventions in its long post-1990 recession. Proposed state actions in today's global recession include "bailouts" of selected industries (especially finance); (re)regulations of enterprises and markets; central bank reductions in interest rates and expansions of money supplies; and federal tax cuts and "stimulus" spending. Such interventions sometimes helped the US through past recessions. They never solved the basic problem of *recurring* recessions.

Class struggles often provoke capitalism's cyclical booms and busts. The more severe recessions bring state interventions and regulations to help capitalists survive capitalism's convulsions. Once the immediate economic crisis is past, capitalists proceed to undo state interventions again. So long as capitalists appropriate surpluses, they always use them to evade, weaken, or destroy state interventions that constrain them. Meanwhile they try to keep public debate and policy away from systemic solutions to recurring recessions.

And so, capitalist cycles recur. Each economic cycle imposes huge painful social costs. In a parallel ideological cycle, most politicians, mass media, and academics swing ridiculously between hyped celebrations of deregulation and (re)regulation as "the solution to our economic problems."

Capitalism's instability is systemic. To address it without considering systemic change is to continue the history of failure to "solve" that instability. Capitalism's core class conflict between workers and boards of directors was never fundamentally changed by state bailouts, (re)regulations, or monetary and fiscal policies. Capitalism's class structure is likewise not *systemically* changed even if we replace boards of directors privately elected by shareholders with boards of state officials instead. State capitalism (USSR), too, not just private capitalism (US), displayed instabilities driven by class conflicts between surplus producers and appropriators. Notwithstanding differences between the instabilities of state and private capitalism, both still yielded inefficiencies and wastes that each so assiduously documented in the other.

One possible systemic change eliminates capitalist class conflict by reorganizing enterprises to position productive workers as their own collective board of directors, thereby removing one key cause of capitalist instability. Such post-capitalist boards' decisions (about technical change, capital accumulation, wages, and so forth) would differ markedly from capitalist boards' decisions. Post-capitalist boards of directors would differ from capitalist boards in their relations to the state as well. A systemically post-capitalist economy would have its instability problems, but they too would differ from capitalism's.

The point is *not* that this systemic change is the only one that could (or could alone) seriously address capitalism's instability. The goal here is to expose the widespread—and politically self-defeating—refusal, even on the left, to acknowledge such systemic causes. The center and the right will forever debate and oscillate between non-systemic causes and policies (bailouts, regulations, stimuli, etc.). The left's unique contribution could and should be to insist that systemic solutions—e.g., changed class structure of enterprises—be part of public discussion and public policy.

GM's Tragedy: The System Strikes Back

5 June 2009

The greatest tragedies among many in the collapse and bankruptcy of General Motors concern what is *not* happening. There are those solutions to GM's problems *not* being considered by Obama's administration. There are the solutions *not* being demanded by the United Autoworkers Union (UAW). There are all the solutions *not* even being discussed by most left commentators on the disaster. Finally there are crucial aspects of GM's demise *not* getting the attention they deserve.

Let's start with an example of the last. For 50 years, the world market for automobiles has grown spectacularly. The company best positioned to have ridden that rising tide to success was GM, the global market leader for most of that time. Instead, GM failed catastrophically. Those responsible, the ones who planned, adjusted, and competed poorly, have a name. They are the corporation's board of directors: the handful of individuals chosen by and responsible to the handful of major GM shareholders. That board and those shareholders proved across decades that they lacked the understanding, vision, and flexibility to succeed. A rising tide is supposed to lift all boats, but GM's captains managed to sink its boat.

President Obama promises *not* to interfere in decisions of the next post-bankruptcy GM board of directors despite the government being GM's largest shareholder. He further promises to quickly sell the government's shares to "re-privatize" GM (he promises the same for collapsed banks, insurance companies, and other corporations revived by infusions of taxpayer money). Obama's plan returns decision-making to the same boards who just brought us the worst economic crash in 75 years.

GM's bankruptcy cuts employees and the wages and benefits of remaining workers. That will further damage already reeling Midwestern states dependent on the auto industry. Were our culture less subservient to capitalist interests and mentalities, the government would have developed—years ago, but certainly during the last crisis-ridden year—major plans to maintain employment and the regional economy by converting closed auto plants into, for example, production of ecologically sensitive mass transportation systems. That would be a growth industry as many regions seek to reduce the ecological damage from private automobile-based transportation systems. Obama supporters talk about such things but his administration does *not* do them.

Likewise the government might have developed programs to utilize closed plants, warehouses, and showrooms to help laid-off workers organize and operate their own enterprises. For a tiny fraction of the billions given to banks, the government could finance such workers using their skills, their largely untapped managerial capabilities, and their knowledge of and commitment to local needs. This, too, is *not* happening.

The UAW no doubt accepted the horrific terms of Obama's GM bankruptcy plan because otherwise bankruptcy threatened even worse for workers. It was "the best deal possible in the circumstances." However, those circumstances could have been different if the UAW and its allies had fought for them earlier. Suppose, for example, that the UAW, other unions, and the political left had fought for and won laws obligating the government to finance massive investments in new enterprises (producing new things and organized in new ways) whenever private capitalists laid off workers in large numbers. Then the UAW would *not* have had to accept the sort of horrific deal Obama and GM just pushed on them. UAW workers would have refused because they would have known the government was obligated to provide them with new jobs, enterprises, and new supports if a bankrupt GM fired them. The government's costs of bailing out GM through bankruptcy would have had to include the expenses of providing the new jobs and supports to fired workers. The government might then have put heavy pressure on GM for a bailout with many fewer lost jobs. In any case, if such laws had been won, UAW members laid off in a bankruptcy would not face unemployment nor would their communities face the devastation now underway.

The point is that nothing in the Obama-GM tragedy was necessary or unavoidable. The political struggles *not* undertaken and the laws *not* passed created the circumstances that drove UAW capitulation to the Obama bankruptcy as their least awful option. Knee-jerk apologists for the status quo are wrong to dismiss talk of what might have been. What might have been— but was not won or even fought for—determines today's mass sufferings as the GM tragedy unfolds. Without past labor-left alliances struggling for laws such as the example above describes, the way was cleared for GM and Washington to devise a choice for the UAW that made its members losers either way.

GM played by the capitalist system's rules. First, it always aimed to profit by driving its employees as hard as possible and paying them as little as it could. Second, GM secured the US market for its cars and trucks by blocking the development of high-quality mass transportation here. Autoworkers fought, through the UAW, and eventually won decent wages and benefits that became goals for all other unions and workers for decades. US citizens' efforts to get quality mass transportation failed (hence Europe's far superior mass transport systems).

Under capitalism's rules, the decent wages and working conditions won by the UAW provoked GM to strike back by moving production where wages and benefits were lower. Thus GM's vehicle production inside the US peaked in the late 1970s (over 6 million) and has since fallen steadily (over 2 million in 2008). GM profited more from the much cheaper labor in China, Brazil, India, and elsewhere. The big losers have been the hundreds of thousands of laid-off, retired, and the few still employed autoworkers, and everyone in Detroit and all the other consequently devastated communities. This week's GM bankruptcy creates still more losers to "rebuild GM's profitability."

Workers who struggle successfully for decent wages and working conditions always find that the system strikes back.

That's how capitalism works, how capitalists profit. Republicans and Democrats alike proudly serve that system. And the lesson for GM and other workers is …?

Crises *in* vs. *of* Capitalism

9 July 2009

Capitalism has generated recurring "crises" everywhere and throughout its history. It alternates bursts of growth and prosperity with crisis periods when many workers lose jobs and homes, bankruptcies close enterprises, production shrinks, and governments reduce public services. Growth periods almost always promote speculation, overproduction, inflation, and excess debts that crises then erase or even reverse. As crises deepen, the increasingly desperate unemployed accept lower wages and poorer working conditions. Business "revives" if and when lower wages and poorer working conditions provide sufficiently attractive profit opportunities for capitalists to resume production and hiring. Crises are thereby overcome. Growth and prosperity return to build toward the next crisis. Capitalism's ups and downs vary in length; their oscillating pattern remains the same.

Crises *in* capitalism (depressions, recessions, cyclical downturns, etc.) are neither new nor unusual. Because capitalism works that way, its supporters came to label the more severe or protracted down periods *crises* because they feared that capitalism's victims would turn against it and seek basic social change. Capitalism's defenders eventually developed a set of policies to manage its inherent economic instability. They include automatic and discretionary "stabilizers" derived from Keynes' Depression-era writings, stimulus and bailout programs, deficit spending, and so on. Past and present advocates of such policies have believed they would both overcome whatever crisis existed then and also prevent future crises. No policies have *ever*, to date, achieved the latter goal. Today's global crisis proves that. Nor is there agreement about whether these policies *ever* overcame a crisis. For example, scholars continue to debate whether FDR's economic policies ended the Great Depression *or* whether it passed because falling wages and business bankruptcies eventually renewed profit opportunities for new investments *or* because of the government's build-up toward World War II.

Political and cultural policies also seek to manage capitalism's recurring crises. FDR thus orchestrated a political New Deal and renewed nationalist cultural themes. These focused attention away from questioning capitalism. Similarly, Pope Benedict's *Charity in Truth* encyclical, released last week, responds to today's crisis by calling for a recommitment in business affairs to Christian values of love, charity, and truth. Crises in capitalism have persisted across all such efforts—economic, political, and cultural—to prevent them. So long as capitalism survives so do its recurring crises.

A crisis *of* capitalism is different. It is not a recurring event. A crisis of capitalism happens when cultural, political, and economic conditions combine to persuade many people that capitalism as a system has outlived its historical usefulness. Seeing it as a barrier to social progress and believing that human communities can organize their economic systems in better, post-capitalist ways, these people begin to move politically. Crises of capitalism may but need not stem from crises in capitalism. For example, potential crises of capitalism loomed at moments in the 1930s and again in the 1960s. The former coincided with a crisis in capitalism; the latter did not. Neither moment had sufficiently extensive support or lasted long enough for those potentials to be realized.

One obstacle preventing crises in capitalism from becoming crises of capitalism is belief that no alternative to capitalism exists. All enterprises are then thought to require the usual division between workers and boards of directors. They must have shareholders electing those boards to hire and fire all employees and make key business decisions alone or with major shareholders. Interactions among businesses, workers, and consumers must happen chiefly by market exchanges. Only then, this belief holds, are modern civilization and standards of living possible. This belief shapes the Obama administration's response to the global crisis.

A more subtle obstacle is belief that an achievable and superior alternative to capitalism exists. That alternative involves larger or smaller shifts from private enterprises to state-regulated or state-owned enterprises, from shareholder-elected boards of directors to state officials (chosen democratically or otherwise) regulating or functioning as such boards, from markets to state-planning as the mechanism to allocate resources and products. However, that alternative largely ignores and so leaves basically unchanged the internal organization of enterprises (whether private or state), their division between the mass of productive employees and the small groups making the decisions about what, how, and where to produce and how to dispose of products and profits. Those small groups have retained their positions either as state-regulated but still private boards of directors, or, under state ownership, as state officials running state enterprises.

Transitions from capitalism to such an alternative have often been understood as transitions to socialism or communism. They repeatedly inspired heroic struggles by capitalism's victims and critics. Those struggles often yielded progressive social changes. Today in many countries important voices propose such transitions in response to the global capitalist crisis.

However, such transitions to socialism and communism have serious contradictions. They distract capitalism's victims and critics from organizational transformations inside enterprises to focus instead on various kinds and degrees of state economic interventions. The distraction secures capitalism's survival in two ways. First, those transitional movements preserve enterprises' internal divisions between employers and employees. Marx emphasized the centrality to capitalism of this relation between two different groups inside each enterprise; he defined "exploitation" as the relation whereby one group, productive laborers, produces a surplus appropriated and distributed by the other. To maintain exploitation inside enterprises (private or state) keeps in place a foundational dimension of capitalism. Second, maintaining exploitation gives the exploiters the incentive and the resources (the surplus they appropriate) to evade, weaken, and eventually eradicate whatever regulations, taxes, and other changes reformers win in responding to any crisis. Thus, in the decades after FDR's economic reforms, US corporate boards of directors utilized the surpluses they appropriated to roll back the New Deal. Similarly, in the 1980s, state officials atop Soviet enterprises utilized the surpluses generated there to roll back the USSR's 1917 transition to socialism.

Two lessons: (1) crises in capitalism will recur until a crisis of capitalism provokes a transition out of capitalism that includes ending exploitation inside enterprises, and (2) the alternative to exploitation requires workers themselves democratically and collectively to appropriate and distribute the surpluses they produce.

2. The Role of Economic Theory

Evangelical Economics

4 January 2006

R ight-wing faith-based politics in the US has its counterpart in faith-based economics. The school of economics that dominates education, journalism, and politics—called "neoclassical" economics—has absolute faith in two secular gods. These are private property and markets. Neoclassical economists believe that these two institutions cause the maximum achievable economic prosperity and progress for all. Alternative schools of economics (Marxian, Keynesian, and so on) are denounced by neoclassicals as heretical and absurd. People persuaded by these alternative schools are ridiculed as wrong, insufficiently trained, or simply stupid. If they persist in the error of their ways, they are said to be driven by sinister, perverse motivations and painted as anti-science, anti-reason, anti-American, anti-prosperity, and so on. The fervor of the neoclassical faithful determines which epithets get hurled (and the speaking opportunities denied, the teaching jobs withheld, etc.).

The first holy institution for neoclassical economics is *private property*, as opposed to the state itself owning or administering socially-owned property or collective property. The second is the *market* (rather than political, cultural, traditional institutions) as the means for distributing resources (land, labor power, and capital) to the producers and distributing products to consumers. Private property owners "freely" buying and selling in markets is what delivers optimum economic performance and results for everyone. The neoclassical faithful praise Adam Smith for the insight that private property plus markets function so perfectly that it seems as though God's "invisible hand" guarantees that everything works out for the very best for all His children.

Right-wing evangelical religionists believe that the good life requires absolute subordination and obedience to their interpretation of God's word. Evangelical economists believe that economic prosperity, efficiency, and progress require the same subordination and obedience to the dictates of private property and markets. Selected Holy books serve evangelicals as final proofs of God's word. Similarly, other selected books—the textbooks summarizing neoclassical economic research—serve neoclassical economists in the same way.

Right-wing evangelicals worry about the Devil who always lurks: the threatening other to be banished, defeated, ostracized, silenced, or converted. For them, the bad are those driven by the Devil to disobey, ignore, or deny God and thereby interfere in his plan for world happiness and salvation. For evangelical economists, the bad are those who lack faith in private property and markets. They disobey—usually by getting the state to disobey—the freedom of markets and the liberties of private property. Thus they interfere in the optimum economic results that would otherwise flow from private property and free markets. The threatening others for neoclassical economics are the "heterodox economists" (the word currently in vogue) who dissent from the neoclassical orthodoxy and thus must be banished, defeated, ostracized, silenced, or converted.

For rightist evangelicals, the sick and the miserable are those whose insufficient faith and resulting bad behavior drew God's punishment. Yet, that punishment is also a merciful test of their faith to see if they can and will repent and thereby emerge from their tribulations. The healthy and prosperous are those who have passed God's tests by means of faith and moral behavior. It follows, for example, that for the state to help the sick and miserable is to interfere in God's will and God's ways, to deprive sinners of the freedom to respond to God's will and pass His tests, which is their only real hope for salvation.

Likewise, for the evangelical economists, if the state helps the unemployed, the poor, etc., it interferes in the workings of private property and markets. That precludes the poor and unemployed from learning and responding to market pressures and signals—passing the market test—that alone can enable them finally and permanently to overcome their economic tribulations (by working, changing jobs, adjusting "lifestyles," learning skills, etc.). In response to markets, the economically "disadvantaged" can pull themselves up by the bootstraps. Only then will they truly emerge from poverty (acquire property). By contrast, state support will only sap their initiative and deepen their culture of poverty and dependence.

The rightist religious evangelicals recognize that sometimes the Devil wins, but just for a while before God returns the faithful to supremacy. Dark times occur when people lose their faith, turn to wicked ways, suffer, and thus are eventually brought back to see God's light. The neoclassicals work a parallel story about how, in the Great Depression of the 1930s, people lost faith in private property and markets. This opened the way for the economic devil—FDR's New Deal state—to interfere with private property and markets according to the statist economics of Mr. Keynes. But the state was eventually recognized as the cause of economic suffering that could only be overcome by returning to full faith in (subordination to) private property and markets. Thus, the right-wing evangelical politician, Bush, made common cause with the evangelical economists for the Great Revival we have today.

The arrogance and intolerance of rightist evangelicals makes them disinterested in the details of the Devil's minions. They lump together atheists, agnostics, and those faithful to other Gods than theirs as all simply evil. The evangelical economists match them by driving from their temples (the schools, the media, and politics) every kind of economist other than the neoclassical. They care little for the difference between Keynesians (who want state interference to save capitalism from the failures of its markets and private property) and Marxists (who think civilization can and should do far better than capitalism). For the neoclassicals, everyone else is dangerous and unacceptable. And so they justify the fact that nearly all economic teaching, publishing, and politics in the US is exclusively neoclassical.

Once again, in the name of absolute truth, dissent and debate are banished as a moral imperative. Until, of course, the next revolution and renaissance of genuinely free thought.

Dedicated to the memory of Harry Magdoff

Flip-Flops of Economics

18 January 2009

Most US economists are professors in colleges and universities. Their academic positions enable research and teaching that is supposed to be independent of corporate interests. They could, at least hypothetically, provide the critical insights into economic problems needed for their solution. Economists might help to propose, evaluate, and debate the wide range of possible solutions—from those that minimally change the status quo to those that entail fundamental social change. However, history shows that most professional economists have been subservient to corporate interests rather than constructive critics. They celebrated capitalism, ignored or dismissed alternative economic systems, and only argued over how best to manage the huge social costs of capitalism's recurring instability. The economists' shameful corporate subservience has been the nation's loss.

The US professional economic establishment—its members call themselves "mainstream"—never leads. It always follows. Before the Great Depression, mainstream economists dutifully embraced what they called "neoclassical economics." This economic "science" showed, they said, that what profited business benefited the whole society. In this mainstream perspective, private enterprise and markets worked best for everyone when left free of government regulation or interference. Big business led and publicly promoted this celebration of capitalism. Colleges and universities sought financial contributions from businesses, their owners, and their leaders. They needed enrollments from these people's children (few others could afford the costs of higher education). Academic administrations neither wanted nor supported professors who criticized private business interests or otherwise displeased them (for example, by challenging mainstream economic science).

After 1929, when private enterprises and free markets yielded the Great Depression, business largely shifted to advocate massive government interventions to "fix" the broken economy (as it does again today). Except for a few diehards, the professional economists quickly followed and reversed their "science." They found a new guru in John Maynard Keynes who extolled the virtues and clarified the mechanisms of government economic interventions. Mainstream economics became Keynesian from the late 1930s through the 1970s. Everywhere college economics courses taught about business cycles (the polite term for capitalism's chronic instability). Textbooks instructed a generation that governments' monetary and fiscal policies were necessary and effective means to limit, offset, and eventually eliminate business cycles.

In the 1970s, the mainstream reversed course yet again. Keynesian economics had failed to overcome or even prevent capitalist business cycles in the US. Monetary and fiscal policies had not delivered the prosperity, growth, and stability promised by the Keynesians. Meanwhile, US corporations had gotten rich and powerful enough—while memories of the Great Depression had faded enough—to undermine the government regulations and controls provoked by the Great Depression. Because business resented those government interventions that limited profits, corporate interests promoted Reagan's candidacy for the presidency. His lifetime service to corporate interests qualified him to roll back the New Deal. Tax cuts, especially on businesses and the rich, and deregulation of business became mantras for leading politicians in both parties. Corporate America resumed the pre-1929 celebration of private enterprise and free markets.

Academic economists again followed. Curricula, textbooks, and conferences all changed. Keynesian economics was out, neoclassical economics was back in, and Milton Friedman was the new guru. He had been a diehard who kept celebrating private enterprise and free markets across the mainstream's Keynesian period. Then, as businesses increasingly decided that "our economy no longer needed government intervention" that constrained profits, Friedman won their support for his University of Chicago economics department. So, in Reagan's new America, the economics profession dutifully found that Friedman's economics was now "correct" and "scientific." He and his supporters took over the mainstream. They marginalized Keynesians and breathlessly re-endorsed the old pre-1929 "neoclassical" economics that exalted private enterprise and free markets as guarantors of prosperity.

So complete was the academic mainstream's embrace of neoclassical economics that very few students learned about capitalism's instability. Courses in business cycles, once staples of the economics curriculum, largely vanished. The Bush government's economists were products of economics educations that incapacitated them to cope with today's massive capitalist crash. Thus, they (1) failed to see, let alone prevent, the crash, (2) waited too long to act as the crash unfolded across the latter part of 2007 and 2008, and (3) proposed one half-baked and ineffective government policy after another beginning in mid-2008. The economists gathered by Obama exemplify the same incapacitated generation.

The profession's shameful history of opportunism may be best illustrated by the January 2009 annual meeting of the supremely mainstream American Economics Association (AEA). Late 2008 had seen big businesses get trillions in government bailouts. Leading mainstream economists at the AEA meeting cravenly announced the errors of their former ways and advocated a return to Keynesian economics. Neoclassical economists saw their careers jeopardized and acted quickly. *New York Times* reporter Louis Uchitelle even applied the religious term "conversion" to the paper by Harvard's Martin Feldstein. Like many born-again Christians, though, born-again Keynesians will no doubt backslide at the first sign of financial-sector stabilization.

To sum up, repeated oscillations between neoclassical and Keynesian economics in defining mainstream economics reveal the profession's opportunistic subservience to business needs. The same subservience explains why it consistently refuses to engage the economists who respond to capitalism's instability by advocating social change to alternative economic systems. In the wake of yet another massive capitalist breakdown, however, our real choices need not and should not be limited to neoclassical or Keynesian economics, to just another shift between private and state-managed forms of capitalism. The case for debating movement beyond capitalism has never been so strong. The now considerable theoretical literature on post-capitalist economies (for example, S. Resnick and R. Wolff, *Class Theory and History: Capitalism and Communism in the USSR*, New York: Routledge, 2002) and the accumulation of local and national experiences with them provide ample resources and lessons to make such moves.

3. Markets and Efficiency

Oil and Efficiency Myths

11 November 2007

Everything Americans do requires transportation because our individualized homes, like our jobs and shopping locations, are all considerable distances from one another except in our largest, densest cities. The private automobile rules. Everything we buy in a store got there by truck. Two-thirds of US oil consumption goes for transportation, most of that for private automobiles. Oil and gasoline prices are key components of our national and personal financial situations much as the production and consumption of oil and gasoline are key causes of environmental damage as well as unnatural death and injury. Mass transportation is minimized in the US and usually starved of financial support where it does exist.

This system, while very profitable for certain industries and enterprises, was never "efficient" unless you equate profitability and efficiency, as if profits measured efficiency. Once you take into account costs not included in corporate accounting, "efficiency" quickly vanishes. Profits are positive for many corporations involved in transportation directly or indirectly, because they do not have to count the costs of death and injury to tens of thousands of families affected by car accidents every year. Even the insurance companies count only what they have to pay for those accidents, which is far different from their life-long costs to those involved. Corporations don't begin to measure, let alone count, all the costs of polluted air, water, and ground. No one factors in the cost of expensive wars such as Iraq undertaken in part to secure the desperately needed oil.

Partly such costs are impossible to measure, since they affect so many people in so many ways and so far into an unknowable future. But they are very real costs. They make the usual claims about the "efficiency" of the private-automobile-based US transportation system and economy at best tragic jokes.

All this comes home more sharply to the American people these days. Crude oil prices are pushing toward $100 per barrel and average regular gasoline prices toward $3 per gallon. In the years 2005, 2006, and 2007, the average increase in all consumer prices other than energy was around 2.5 percent per year, while over the same time the average annual increase in oil prices was over 12 percent (5 *times as fast*) and the average annual increase in gasoline prices was over 10 percent. In simplest terms, oil and gas prices are now draining money out of US consumers. They have less to spend on everything else. And their reduced spending means that those consumers are now driving the US economy downward toward recession.

The rising oil prices also affect us by altering the international political scene, giving nations like Saudi Arabia, Venezuela, and Russia, among others, the freedom and resources to pursue their interests far more aggressively than would otherwise be the case. Rising oil prices elsewhere fuel virtual civil wars (for example, in Nigeria and Iraq) that affect us all in many ways. Rising oil prices and their political consequences are yet other uncounted costs of the US dependence on oil.

And make no mistake, the US dependence on oil is key to what happens in the world oil market, including what happens to oil prices. With our 2.4 percent of the world's people, the US consumes about 25 percent of the world's oil. And 60 percent of what we consume comes from elsewhere. The US uses 2.9 gallons of oil per day per person; the global average is 0.5 gallons; and in the rest of the industrialized world, the usage is 1.3 gallons per day. The US shapes the world oil market more than any other country does.

Other nations' reliance on mass transportation systems is the main reason they use so much less oil per person. The "efficiency" of a US transportation system based on private individual vehicles has produced its extraordinary level of dependency on oil and on the world oil market. So of course the war in Iraq has something to do with oil.

The US economy was built upon and around the private automobile mode of transportation. The new suburban reconfiguration of our population's residential location after World

War II enabled a housing boom, a shopping revolution, a vast infrastructure investment program built around road systems, and so on. The corporations profiting from all that spending successfully blocked and undercut all alternative modes of transportation or home-building or community construction ever since. They pressed for (bought) government policies to the same ends.

The entire system now dependent on oil requires a systematic response if the immense costs and risks of oil dependency are to be overcome. No small, piecemeal solutions will work. None of those so far tried by politicians eager to appear focused on the problem have worked. So the situation has kept deteriorating (except, of course, for those profiting from it all).

But perhaps now the situation will change. Because finally corporate America is getting worried (at least those parts hurt by the oil situation). The largest single employer in the US, Wal-Mart, has been blaming its poor sales records in several recent quarters on the problem that its shoppers spent so much on oil and gas that they had to reduce expenditures at the store. Perhaps the whole retail industry will go to work, round up other corporate allies, and demand concessions from those corporations profiting from oil dependency. Maybe such a falling out among corporations can do what a disorganized and demoralized mass population could not.

But then a depressing prospect likely opens up yet again. The "solution" that emerges from struggles among private corporate enterprises will likely once again accommodate their profit concerns at the expense of the mass population, which is neither consulted nor allowed to participate in making the key decisions. So it was before and so it will be again unless and until a mass movement arises to demand and obtain real democratic participation and control over solving the mess left by "efficient private enterprise."

The Rating Horrors & Capitalist "Efficiency"

4 January 2008

Many aspects of our "efficient" capitalism combined to produce the credit meltdown that now threatens ever more aspects of the global economy. One was the private rating companies' failure to accurately assess and honestly reveal the risks of securities based on a "bundle" of loans (securities that provide their owners with a portion of that bundle's principal and/or interest). This was especially true for securities based on mortgage loans issued in the go-go years of the housing boom. Investors around the world bought those securities based on those companies' ratings. Their purchases financed the US housing bubble now gone bust. We know now that those ratings were badly mistaken. Owners of those securities around the globe are taking staggering losses and reducing their lending to all borrowers. Anxiety about the risks of *all sorts* of borrowing has risen alongside deepening distrust of all risk assessments. Defaults, bankruptcies, and foreclosures rise together with the odds of recession in 2008.

Understanding why the rating companies contributed to this disaster opens a crucial window into today's global credit crisis. It also teaches basic lessons about today's globalized capitalism. Step one is to grasp the structure of the industry that sells assessments of the risks attached to securities (including those based on loans). Of the 150 rating enterprises around the world, three dominate. Moody's and Standard and Poor's—the two industry giants—have an 80 percent market share. The US Justice Department refers quaintly to them as a "partner monopoly." Fitch has between 10 and 15 percent, and all the others share what remains. This industry structure generates massive profits and profit rates at the top. Moody's, for example, generated 2006 revenues of $2 billion, from which it derived a pre-tax income of $1.1 billion (a better than 50 percent profit rate). No wonder that Moody's top shareholder (a 19 percent stake) is Warren Buffett. That wizard was wise enough to buy

Moody's but not the securities that Moody's rated. Then again, his company, Berkshire-Hathaway, apparently held on to those shares as the credit disaster drove them down from over $70 to under $35 across 2007.

Step two is to see how badly those companies failed. Consider the research undertaken by Morgan Stanley and described in a recent (24 December 2007) *Barron's Magazine* article. They studied the 6,431 sub-prime residential mortgage-backed securities issued in 2006. Of these, 2,087 issues were rated AAA (the highest rating, the lowest risk); 1,266 were rated AA; and the rest were rated A or lower. Within one year of being issued, most of these securities were reexamined by the rating companies as the values of such securities tumbled and it became clear that the rating process had missed something. As a result of their reexamination, over 50 percent were down-graded, i.e. given a new, lower rating. Morgan Stanley compared the rate of downgrades in 2006–2007 to the historical norm for 1998–2006. The results are stunning. Among AAA-rated sub-prime residential mortgage-backed securities, 4 percent were downgraded (whereas the historical norm was 0.12 percent). Among AA rated securities, 12.2 percent were downgraded (versus an historical norm of 0.64 percent). Of securities rated A and below, some 97 percent experienced downgrades (versus the historical norm of 1.24 percent).

Step three is to see the ramifications of so spectacular a failure. Across the world, all sorts of individuals, enterprises, governments, and non-governmental organizations (universities, charities, hospitals, etc.) purchased these securities to fund their activities. They now have to downgrade their activities to accommodate their now-downgraded investments, their lost billions. We have not yet begun to count the social costs of downgraded activities. Moreover, it is too soon to take a real count. All we can be sure of is that the losses are enormous. As risk aversion spreads, holders of other debt-backed securities lose more billions. Those with debts find it harder or impossible to turn over those debts. New borrowers face higher costs for smaller loans requiring higher down payments. Economic activity shrinks. The US housing industry is thus already a disaster.

Some losses and some shrinkages have been announced. Many are yet unknown, uncounted, or else hidden, because if known they would be politically explosive. For example, what losses on such securities would the Chinese government have to admit to its people? How will governors and mayors cope with US voters' anger at property tax increases required to compensate for looming difficulties in issuing bonds rated by the same, now-compromised rating companies? Which pension funds suffered losses from such securities that may prevent them from fully paying promised benefits? Which mutual funds purchased mortgage-backed securities and have yet to count or announce all the losses? Which of those mutual funds are included in the portfolios that your life depends on, directly or indirectly? What happens now that the companies who insure loans lack sufficient funds to pay the claims coming their way? Are the sub-prime credit card, student, and corporate loans that back many billions in other securities about to implode too?

During 2007, repeated scares about imported Chinese products (pet food, toys, etc.) taught us the lesson that the private profit motive can throw many toxic commodities onto global markets. The sub-prime mortgage scandals teach the lesson that the financial industries can spew even more toxic products onto global markets. The rating horrors teach that the profit motive can also infect the enterprises charged specifically with assessing the risk of those financial products. Along the way, huge profits have been made—one side of the coin—as huge numbers have been and will be fleeced—the other side.

Ratings themselves were initially reforms. Years ago, when huge losses flowed from securities whose issuers had misrepresented their risks, the reformist demand arose that someone should "independently" assess their risk so investors would be honestly informed. It turns out now that providers of such independent assessments can misrepresent them as disastrously as their issuers did and do. Yet another set of such reforms—and that is all the *Barron's* article cited above offers—promises no better success than past reforms. Moreover, governmental "independent risk assessments" are as corruptible as their private enterprise counterparts.

The *Barron's* article uses the word "rotten" to describe the sub-prime mortgage crisis. Perhaps that word describes something deeper at work in our economic system that keeps regenerating booms and bubbles exhibiting irrational exuberance and gross financial hustles. At what point do the resulting vast economic and social losses require us to look deeper at more fundamental changes?

Market Terrorism

23 March 2008

The intimate partnership between mainstream economics and right-wing ideology has long trumpeted the wonderful efficiency of markets. In these partners' fantasy, markets are truly wondrous coordination mechanisms that perfectly match the supply of goods and services to what buyers demand. All this happens, they say with immense self-satisfaction, without the intervention of any government or collective authority (which would, they insist darkly, abuse the power to make such interventions). It must be difficult for these partners now to contemplate how markets first produced and then spread the current financial disasters across the globe.

US markets began the process in 2000 by rapidly generating many more home mortgages and mortgage-backed securities than before. Profit-driven mortgage brokers greatly increased the number of home mortgages. Profit-driven banks saw huge fees in converting these mortgages into securities and selling them to investors in financial markets around the world. To do that, the banks entered the market for security ratings and paid the providers of these, corporations like Moody's and Standard and Poor's, to supply high ratings. The rating companies complied and made huge profits in that market. The banks also purchased insurance policies ("guaranteeing" these mortgage-backed securities' principal and interest payments) in the market for them. The insurance companies made much money selling those policies.

No conspiracy was needed to produce the real estate bubble, nor its current, devastating implosion. Just the normal workings of profit-driven markets sufficed to do the job.

Meanwhile, the labor market in the US since 2000 kept real wages from rising. So, many workers could not keep up their mortgage payments, especially when the market prices for food and fuel soared. They stopped their mortgage payments. The banks, hedge funds, and others who had purchased the highly-rated, insured mortgage-backed securities discovered that the market had sold them bad investments. Trying to sell these bad investments, they discovered that there were few buyers. Mortgage-backed securities' prices collapsed. That's how markets work. The lowered prices of mortgage-backed securities reduced the wealth of the banks, hedge funds, and other investors around the world who still owned them. The collapsing market for mortgage-backed securities commenced to terrorize all the world's financial movers and shakers starting in the second half of 2007.

When banks, hedge funds, and wealthy investors get hurt, they immediately use markets to try to shift the pain onto others. Banks sought to recoup losses from their bad investments by withdrawing credit from individuals and businesses and/or charging more for the loans they provided to them. In economic language, the mortgage-backed securities' collapse was spread to the credit markets generally. And that brought the disaster to credit-dependent individuals and businesses that had had nothing to do with mortgages or real estate. The market mechanism thus spread terror to vast new populations.

As credit markets extended the mortgage-backed securities disaster, via constricted credit to other borrowers, those borrowers had in turn to reduce their purchases in the consumer and capital goods markets. The linked markets proved to be a very effective mechanism enabling the mortgage-backed security crisis to provoke an economy-wide recession in the United States. Since the US is the largest market in the world for commodities produced everywhere, its recession will spread—by means of the market—to produce economic turmoil and suffering globally. The world's markets comprise a terror network, a system for producing economic disaster and delivering it to every corner of the planet.

Much like other kinds of religious fundamentalism, *market fundamentalism*—the dogma that markets guarantee efficiency and prosperity—has wrecked economies and lives. Plato and Aristotle explained the dark side of markets thousands of years ago. They and countless others since then have shown how and why markets repeatedly destroy the bonds of community and undermine social cohesion. Yet the market fundamentalism of recent decades blinded leaders and many followers to the known failures of markets. They and we will now pay a heavy price for their blindness.

I am not saying that markets must never be used as ways to distribute some products and some productive resources. That would simply be a reverse fundamentalism. Rather, let's recognize that markets have strengths and weaknesses and act accordingly. Just as we know government intervention and planning needs checks and balances to avoid its pitfalls, markets need all sorts of checks and balances to avoid their horrors. The worship of markets "free" from constraints and controls is bad witchcraft the world can no longer afford.

In any case, markets, whether controlled more or less, are not our economy's only basic problem. How markets work is shaped by how we organize production. Our economic system organizes production in ways that do more damage than markets. Production occurs mostly in corporations run by boards of directors (usually 15–20 individuals). Those boards receive the profits made from the goods and services produced by the workers. Those boards decide what to do with those profits. Those boards manipulate markets to enhance their profits and to maintain their position atop the corporate system. In contrast, the workers—the majority in every enterprise—do not get the profits their labor produces nor have they any say in what is done with them. In the market as organized by boards of directors, workers get too little in wages and pay too much in prices.

This system places conflict and conflict of interests right in the heart of production. Boards of directors work to get more out of workers while paying them less; the workers want the opposite. What a way to organize production!

Class conflict on the job spills over into markets. "Reforms" imposed on markets in the wake of their current meltdown will fail if we do not change the organization of production. Suppose we reorganized production so that those who produce the goods are also those who receive the profits and decide on their use. Suppose in this way US workers achieve what polls show they want—to be their own bosses on the job. Suppose every job description obliges the worker holding that job to participate in collective discussion and decision on how to use the enterprise's profits.

As their own bosses, workers could effectively insist that markets be just as controlled and limited to serve the majority as corporations and governments should be.

4. Wages, Productivity, and Exploitation

US Pensions: Capitalist Disaster

19 December 2005

The US pension systems for workers are now widespread disasters. Many corporations and many cities and states lack the money to pay all the benefits they have promised and legally owe to present and future retirees. Estimates of the shortfall range around $450 billion in the private sector plus at least another $300 billion in the public sector. Retired workers with lost or reduced pensions suffer extra strain on family and household finances. Millions now working expect pension reductions will be added to the overwork and over-indebtedness that burden them. Not only for them does disaster loom; reduced pensions will directly undercut an economy that has become increasingly dependent on consumer expenditures.

The issue is, at bottom, remarkably simple. Private corporations initially established pensions to enhance profits. They aimed to reduce the costs of employee turnover by offering pensions to workers who stayed until retirement. In bargaining with unions, many corporations offered workers less in wage increases and more in pension "improvements." After all, pensions not only reduced labor turnover costs immediately, but they would only cost the corporations later when workers retired. Unions often accepted labor contracts with less wage gains in exchange for pensions promising security for retirement years. Of course, once pensions were established, corporations sought to shift their costs to workers.

Pensions arose in and because of the endless struggle among employers and workers over wages and profits. Pension benefits altered over the years as that struggle continued under changed conditions. And, today, the same struggle confronts workers with the prospect of employers ending pensions altogether.

Particularly after World War II, pensions were won by many unions whose members' memories of the Great Depression made pensions very attractive. Several large corporations agreed to establish them (notably Ford and General Motors), but often reluctantly and only if they got wage "concessions" in return.

However, once pensions were established, corporations discovered many ways to "underfund" them (the polite word for not setting aside enough money to pay for the promised pensions or mismanaging investments made with that money). When this became a public issue (especially after Studebaker's 1963 collapse deprived its workers of their pensions), the response was neither strict controls over corporations nor strict punishments for their mismanagement of pension funding. Instead, in 1974, Congress passed the Employment Retirement Income Security Act (ERISA) that established little real control while setting up the Pension Benefit Guarantee Corporation (PBGC). The PBGC is a government insurance company that is supposed to pay promised pensions when corporations fail to provide enough money for them.

It should come as no surprise that ERISA was full of carefully crafted loopholes that allowed more, not less, corporate underfunding of pensions—nicely documented in Roger Lowenstein's "The End of Pensions" in the *New York Times* (30 October 2005). So, today, corporations have underfunded their pensions by hundreds of billions. Therefore, their workers will suffer reduced support in their retirement or else Washington will have to shift billions to the PBGC so it can pay pensions for the corporations. If such billions are taken from other programs, workers will likely suffer reduced social services. If such billions come from higher taxes, we need to remember who will actually pay most of such extra taxes. The fact is that US corporations have steadily shifted most of their federal tax burdens onto US households: around 1970 corporate profit taxes contributed almost 20 percent of the federal government's tax revenues, whereas in the early years of this century it hovered around 7 percent. Over the same period, wealthy households have likewise shifted much of their federal income tax burden onto middle- and lower-income households: top income tax rates fell by half; dividend, estate, and capital gains taxes fell substantially; while payroll tax rates on wages and salaries doubled.

Since the Bush regime leaders (and their Democratic counterparts) refuse to demand pension reparations from corporations, the private-sector pension disaster presents this choice: (1) cut pension benefits and thereby condemn private-sector retirees to financial difficulty, poverty, or becoming burdens on their families after a lifetime of labor; or (2) give the vast majority of already stressed households reduced federal programs and/or new tax bills. The corporations win either way; and the working class loses either way. Sound familiar?

Nor is the situation much different for government employees working for states, cities, and towns. There, politicians have offered public employees relatively generous pension benefits in exchange for their votes. Such deals benefit politicians in two ways. First, they can avoid tax increases now because the costs of pension benefits happen in the future when they hope to be in higher political positions. Second, because of remarkably loose accounting rules, politicians could do just what the corporate executives did, namely underfund the pensions for public employees. To pay for the legally mandated public pensions, eventually the states, cities, and towns will have to raise taxes or cut their spending on other public programs and services. Given the politicians' fears of taxing corporations or the wealthy or of cutting state programs benefiting them, the costs of the public pension disaster will also fall on workers.

First results of the unfolding disaster are already here. Fearing that a desperate population might eventually demand that *they* actually pay for promised pensions, corporations are ending pensions, often by not offering them to new employees. In 1980, roughly 40 percent of private-sector jobs had pension benefits; today less than 20 percent do. Major US corporations with unfunded pension obligations (including, for example, Delta Airlines, Delphi Corporation, Bethlehem Steel, and Northwest Airlines) have increasingly used bankruptcy laws to avoid them (i.e., shift them onto the PBGC). Other companies face situations not so different from that of Ford Motor Company whose unfunded pension obligations as of December 31, 2003, totaled $11,689,000,000, while the total value of Ford Motor Company on that date was $89,000,000 *less* than that (Bernard Condon, "The Coming Pension Crisis," *Forbes Magazine*, 12 August 2004). Yet the PBGC cannot pay for present— let alone anticipated future—failures by private corporations to pay their pension obligations. The PBGC already has a deficit exceeding $30 billion. Without the money it needs to pay for the pensions it insured, the PBGC will now likely add new demands on federal tax revenues.

In the public sector, Alaska has responded to unfunded pension obligations to its employees by deciding to offer future public employees there no pensions at all. Michigan made similar moves, and other states may follow their examples. The immense scope of underfunded pension obligations to municipal employees is only beginning to be measured and understood—to the terror of local politicians and local economies.

The neoliberal age we are declining through displays many new policies, programs, and laws pursued without regard to their future social burdens. These include, alongside the pension disasters, transforming the US from the world's major creditor into its major debtor, despoiling the environment, working families taking on historically unprecedented levels of personal debt, increasing the US trade deficit, and cutting public services. Promoted as "components of an ownership society" or "efficiency-driven" or "required to compete in the world economy," what these policies and programs share is the short-run boost they provide to corporate profits and political careers. The watchword of this age seems to be "grab it all now; who knows or cares what deluge may follow." Thus, to cite yet another example, the underfunding of pensions is small compared to the underfunding of private sector retirees' health plans (see the December 19, 2005 *Business Week* story: "America's Other Pension Problem").

Pensions have represented important hopes, expectations, and investments for millions of workers. In the endless struggles between those who produce the profits and those who receive and disperse them, corporate and political leaders "managed" pension programs into disastrous dead ends. Should we expect anything different from new laws, new accounting rules, and new policies for the PBGC so long as those endless struggles continue? Solving the pension disaster requires something altogether different. If the producers of profits were themselves to appropriate and disperse the profits—if workers were collectively their own bosses—then we might realistically expect pensions to adequately serve their intended beneficiaries.

The Fallout from Falling Wages

12 June 2006

Real wages in the US rose during every decade from 1830 to 1970. Then this central feature of US capitalism stopped, as the figures below show:

1964	$302.52
1974	314.94
1984	279.22
1994	259.97
2004	277.57

Source: Labor Research Associates of New York based on data from the US Department of Labor, Bureau of Labor Statistics; weekly wages expressed in constant 1982 dollars.

No comparable steady rise in real wages has occurred since. The most recent data from the Bureau of Labor Statistics indicate real weekly wages declined again over the last year (2005–2006). American workers' reactions to this downtrend in real wages have profoundly shaped the nation's economy and society for the last thirty years.

Stagnant or falling real wages undermine workers' basic expectations of rising levels of consumption. Those expectations had become key parts of what it meant to be "an American." Rising consumption has long functioned as the evidence of success in achieving the American dream. When, after the mid-1970s, real wages no longer allowed for rising consumption, wage-earners turned, with growing urgency, toward other ways and means to maintain rising consumption. This delayed the inevitable, a falling standard of living, but at great economic and social cost.

In one "solution" to counteract the problem of shrinking real wages, many families sent more members out to work more hours. Part-timers switched to full-time positions or else multiplied part-time jobs to secure more income. Full-timers took second and third jobs. While this helped, in part, to offset the real wage problem, it also disorganized family and household life. Time with spouse and children was cut. So too was the energy and attention adults could devote after work to cope with family problems aggravated by lengthening work times for family members. Rising divorce rates, intra-familial difficulties and abuse, and indices of psychological depression became signs of the costs of this partial "solution." When mothers' entry into the paid workforce required costly daycare for dependents and commercially prepared foods, families again confronted insufficient funds to enable increased consumption.

A second "solution"—when longer work hours did not generate enough money to increase consumption—was to borrow. Multiple credit cards per family and increasing mortgages added to vehicle financing to generate historically unprecedented levels of total consumer debt across the last 25 years—and especially since 2000. March and April 2006 saw negative real savings rates for the public of 1.5 percent. Nor do these stark statistics count the vast sums that adult children increasingly "borrow" from their parents' savings.

Not surprisingly, the debt service portion of disposable income has also reached historic heights. Over 15 percent of after-tax personal income repays debt (despite current low interest rates). Borrowing has thus heaped the costs and anxieties of debt on top of those flowing from increased external work time by family members. The resulting stress levels contributed to the deepening reliance of millions of Americans on legal and illegal drugs, as well as excess food (the "obesity problem") and alcohol. As constricted consumption provoked more work and debt, the latter provoked more consumption as a coping mechanism. More malls filled with more people who increasingly cannot afford to shop there.

Stagnant or falling real wages were partly caused by technological changes and immigration. The former reduced the demand for labor while the latter increased its supply: a combination resulting in predictable downward pressures on wages. Yet immigration receives far more emphasis than rigorous analysis warrants. Other causes of the real wage downtrend were simultaneously its effects: declining union membership and militancy, declining government services and supports to wage-earners, and declining civic (including electoral) participation by the general population. In genuine desperation, a portion of the increasingly stressed, decreasingly organized, and less community-engaged population turned for support and help toward fundamentalist religion. Underfunded and less and less functional government agencies and the Democratic Party associated with them lost considerable public support. Republicans saw their chance to take power. They positioned themselves as the way to (1) bring the change ever more workers felt they needed, (2) restore badly strained "families and family values," and (3) support religious institutions as public service providers. While the Republicans thereby won elections, their free market programs (tax cuts, public service cuts, government deregulation, etc.) never stopped the basic downward cycle of real wages, more work, and higher debt. Predictably, Republicans now face rising problems in sustaining a public perception of economic progress or well-being.

Fundamentalist economic theory accompanied all these developments, the "scientific assurance" to the population that only good things would result from free market programs. That is, "economics" taught the absolute wisdom of cutting taxes, public service delivery, and welfare, as well as removing government controls and regulations of business. Economics *promised* that the resulting inequalities of wealth and income would provide the incentives and capital for greater economic growth beneficial to all.

Economics *proved* that the outsourcing of jobs, greater immigration, and huge federal budget and foreign trade deficits all brought net social benefits and so were best left unimpeded by any government action. In fact, the economics profession has debated these issues for the last 200 years *without resolution among the contending theories and their analyses.* But that fact got swept aside by the Republican need for one absolute version of "economics" that either denied economic problems existed or else glossed them with a scientific guarantee of imminent, free market solutions.

Bush's recent loss of public approval may signal the limits to the last 25 years of economic change and policy. A vast outrage may arise among Americans who "forget" their beliefs in and complicity with policies that are now becoming exposed as failures and who will insist that they were duped and mislead. Then the political pendulum can swing as far toward government economic intervention as earlier it swung the other way. Such shifts have, after all, happened many times in the past. "Economic science" may yet again be reformulated in Keynesian or "socialist" terms to justify such shifts (note Latin America's recent dramatic moves away from its extreme neoliberal policies after the 1970s).

The key questions for many now are (1) how much longer can the combination of real wage decline, rising work effort, debt, and family stress, and deepening social inequalities continue; (2) what might enable Bush & Co. nonetheless to continue the economic direction they champion; and (3) how fast and how far will the backlash proceed if they cannot do so? For socialists, the key political question is different. When private capitalism à la Bush hits its crisis, will the chief socialist response be (as it mostly was after 1929) to support a government intervention aimed to save the system by making it more worker-friendly for a while, until the crisis passes? Or will they demand far more basic economic change?

Reaping the Economic Whirlwind

10 August 2006

Consider these basic facts about the US economy today. First, real hourly wages *fell*, on average, between the first quarter of 2005 and the first quarter of 2006. At the same time, the productivity of those workers *rose*. No advanced degree is required to grasp what's happening here: workers who produced more output this year than last are getting paid less than last year. Workers were not only denied any of the extra output they produced, but their reward for increased productivity was to get even less than they did before they became more productive.

But before we examine who got the fruits of increased productivity plus the fruits of paying less to the more productive workers, let's look at the official numbers provided by the US Labor Department's Bureau of Labor Statistics. US workers' average "real" hourly compensation—where "real" simply means that their money wages are adjusted for the prices workers have to pay—fell by 0.9 percent from the first quarter of 2005 to the same period in 2006. Over the exact same time, labor productivity rose 2.5 percent. From a longer, ten-year perspective, the story is, if anything, more dramatic. Real non-farm hourly compensation (expressed in constant 1982 dollars) was $7.56 in June 1996, rose to $8.32 in June 2002, and retreated to $8.17 in June 2006. That works out to an increase of 8 percent in US workers' average real hourly wages across the last 10 years. During the same decade, productivity rose *at least five times faster*.

The first response to these numbers is "Wow!" The appropriate next step is to grasp the meaning of this growing gap between what workers produce and what they get.

To do this, let's divide employees into two sorts: producers (those who actually make what businesses sell) and enablers (those who secure the context for production: the managers, secretaries, record keepers, security guards, work-site cleaners, lawyers, etc.). Let's also divide the revenues of most businesses into their three basic uses: (1) to replenish tools, equipment, and raw materials used up in production, (2) to pay the wages, salaries and bonuses of all employees, and (3) to deliver profits to the board of directors for their disposition.

The BLS numbers then tell the following story. First, the average real wages of both producing and enabling workers rose very modestly across the last decade, while the volume of goods and services they combined to produce rose *many times faster*. Much more was produced for businesses to sell, so they reaped much greater sales revenues. The BLS wage numbers show that those businesses used very little of those extra sales revenues to pay their workers. So we need to ask and answer the question: to whom did all those extra sales revenues go? Who got that money?

The two clear winners from the last decade's combination of fast-rising productivity and stagnant real wages are those people who actually got the extra business sales revenues that resulted from than combination. The first group is the top set of enablers: the top corporate managers who have taken immense increases in salaries, bonuses, and other parts of their "pay packages" from the increased revenues of the businesses they manage. The second group is the set of those who get direct gains from rising business profits. When businesses have more products to sell while paying most workers little or none of the resulting extra revenues, the result is a boom in business profits. Corporate boards of directors use those profits to pay greater dividends to shareholders, to buy other businesses, to expand their businesses, etc. Rising dividends benefit share-holders, while business growth usually drives up share prices (yielding "capital gains") and that also benefits shareholders.

So there really is no mystery at all about what is happening to the US economy or why it is happening. Because those— the vast majority—who do most of the work to produce rising output don't get most of that extra output, a relatively tiny minority gathers it all in. That is why every measure of the US economy has been showing a rapidly widening gap between the rich and the poor.

Nor is there any real mystery about how workers have managed to keep their consumption rising over the last decade even as their real wages went nowhere. According to US Census Bureau data, during the last decade, average household consumption likely increased about 25 percent. Clearly, that increase could not have been paid for by real wages since they rose only 8 percent. The mystery begins to dissolve once we note that over the last decade US households have sent more members out to work more jobs and longer hours to pay for household consumption. The mystery dissolves completely once we note the simultaneous, massive explosion of household/consumer debt. Because most US workers got little or no real wage increases and because they could not or would not correspondingly curtail their consumption, they had to work more, borrow more, and stress more.

Wage stagnation, debt explosion, stress, and widening wealth and income inequality are now basic pillars of the US economy. And if you sow the wind....

Our Sub-Prime Economy

10 October 2007

What matters most in economics often gets the least attention. So it is with the link between wages and productivity: what workers get paid versus the value of what they produce. Most commentators focus elsewhere. They hype what their employers want to see or what they want others to believe. Stock boosters see market upswings underway or around the corner. Politicians *in power* repeat what the stock boosters say. Those betting on market downturns pay their commentators to pitch gloom and doom. Politicians *out of power* copy them and promise when elected to resume prosperity so they too can mimic the stock boosters.

Let's do the basic US wage and productivity numbers that seem to elude most commentators. The data comes from the US Bureau of Labor Statistics, gathered and interpreted by the Economic Policy Institute (see www.epi.org/datazone).

From 1973 to 2005, this is what happened to the 80 percent of US workers in non-supervisory jobs. Their hourly wages—adjusted for inflation and expressed in 2005 dollars—rose from $15.76 to $16.11. That is, over a 32-year period, most US workers enjoyed a stunning 2 percent increase in what their hourly pay could buy. Because their work weeks shortened over those years, their real weekly pay—what they could actually afford for a week's pay—actually fell from $581.67 to $543.65, a *decline* of 6.5 percent. This means that workers' wages could buy less in 2005 than in 1973.

Over the same thirty years, US workers produced 75 percent more. In the language of economics, that's how much output per worker—"productivity"—rose. Corporations got 75 percent more goods and services produced per worker. They sold that extra output and thus got much more revenue and profit per worker employed. Yet what they paid those workers did not rise. Stagnant wages did not allow the workers to buy any of the extra output they produced.

Why and how did this happen? Over the last three decades, jet travel, computers, the internet, and cell phones changed every workplace on the planet. Companies survived global competition if they produced more with fewer workers. So they changed technology to replace people with machines, and they successfully pressured the remaining employees to work harder and faster. At the same time, they moved production to places where they could minimize costs by using dangerous technologies and production methods (think lead-contaminated toys or chemically dangerous pet food and so on). Perhaps they bribed or persuaded local authorities to ignore the resulting ecological, safety, and health problems; perhaps they just looked the other way as in "failing to properly supervise." In any case, what mattered and what happened was that productivity rose.

Wages, however, went nowhere because US corporations (1) outsourced what had been US jobs to cheap labor overseas, (2) imported immigrants willing to work for less, (3) threatened to export their jobs if US workers pushed wages higher, and (4) financed politicians who legalized all these actions and undercut the already shrinking unions. In 1973, union contracts covered about 24 percent of US non-supervisory workers. By 2005, that number fell to 12.5 percent.

And always, a growing army of well-paid commentators in the mass media glorified the "efficiency of the world economy." Sometimes, troubling facts arose to threaten the constant celebration (anti-free-trade protests, scandals involving toxic exports, etc.). The commentators found ways to ignore them, deflect attention from them, and soothe their audiences by recalling the wonders of "the new modern economy."

Yet the importance of rising worker output coupled with stagnant real wages is clear for anyone willing to see. It is exploitation getting worse. The huge size of the post-1975 productivity-wage gap overwhelms all the usual quibbles about the statistics. The gap between the standard of living that their rising productivity made possible and the standard of living their wages could afford got wider every year.

Many problems unfolding now in the US economy flow from this worsening exploitation. American families, culturally accustomed to measuring individual success by achieved levels of consumption, experienced a thirty-year freeze on how much their wages could buy. Had they limited purchases to that income, they could not have realized the American dream of a rising standard of living. They would have been losers.

So they rebelled. With their wages effectively frozen and no union, party, or social movement available to unfreeze them, workers responded individually. Women moved massively to add wage-labor to their housework. Families undertook massive personal debt. As families and finances became shaky, anxieties grew. Upset by frightening changes on so many levels, Americans sought reassurance or escapes from new pressures. Fundamentalisms enjoyed revivals: in churches, synagogues, and mosques but also in politics, patriotism, "family values," and economics. Escapisms bloomed—spectator sports, drugs, alcohol, food, but also fitness, pornography, and the private techno-worlds of iPods, blogs, chat rooms.

Sub-prime is a euphemism that applies to much more than low-grade mortgage loans. It describes the whole US economy that came *after* the 1945–1975 period, *after* the nation's experiments with a welfare state, a mass middle class, and rising mass consumption. The numbers on productivity and real wages *before* then—from 1945 to 1975—were very different. Productivity rose much faster then than afterward. But the big difference is what happened to real wages: hourly, they rose 75 percent from 1947 to 1972, while weekly they rose 61 percent. In other words, US workers wages then rose with their higher productivity—exactly what *stopped* happening after the mid-1970s.

The welfare state economy of 1945 to 1975 was driven by two interconnected fears: of lapsing back into the Great Depression and of succumbing to socialism. History reduced those fears enough so that, after 1975, business could undo the New Deal and go back to the pre-1929 gaps between rich and poor. Most paid commentators cheer the business reaction as if it were good for everyone, but workers suffering the new sub-prime economy may reckon differently. The explosion of workers' debts has postponed that reckoning. So too have fundamentalism, escapism, and the noise from all those commentators.

How long this sub-prime economy continues depends much more on workers' responses than on Fed policy, dollar depreciation, or tight credit. However, grasping that dependence requires that we disconnect from that other world created and sustained by business and their commentators and politicos.

5. Housing and Debt

Personal Debts and US Capitalism

15 October 2005

There is no precedent in US—or any other—history for the level of personal debt now carried by the American people. Consider the raw numbers. In 1974, Federal Reserve data show that US mortgage plus other consumer debt totaled $627 billion. By 1994, the total debt had risen to $4,206 billion, and by 2004, it reached $9,709 billion. For the second quarter of 2005, the Fed announced that the nation's debt service ratio (debt payments as a percentage of after-tax income) was 13.6 percent, the highest since the Fed began recording this statistic in 1980. Past borrowing now costs Americans so much in debt service that more borrowing is required to maintain, let alone expand consumption.

These facts raise two questions: what caused this mountain of debt to arise and what are its consequences? Answering these questions is an urgent matter since, as has been known for centuries, the risks of high debt include economic collapse.

Since the real wages of most workers stagnated or fell since 1975, they responded partly by borrowing to maintain or raise their living standards. Over the last 25 years, ever more enterprises (stockbrokers, insurance companies, lending branches of industrial corporations, etc.) are seeking high profits by offering easier loans (credit cards, basic mortgages, home equity lines, mortgage refinancing, tax-refund advances, etc.). After the stock market bubble burst in 2000, the Federal Reserve tried to contain the damage by drastic, sustained cuts in interest rates. Already debt-addicted, US households responded to cheap, available credit by borrowing much more.

Historically low interest rates and intense competition among lenders drew millions of Americans into borrowing to buy a first home. Not only the native-born exchanged rental apartments for "the American dream." Millions of immigrants borrowed to partake of that dream too. Millions of other Americans borrowed for costly home expansions and renovations.

The resulting boom in residential construction and its dependent industries partly offset the depressive economic effects of the stock market bubble burst in 2000. A stock market bubble gave way to a housing bubble. As housing prices were bid up, homeowners' "equity" in houses rose, and that allowed them to borrow still more with their higher "home equity" as collateral.

In all debt-based economic upswings, the crucial issue is: How long will lenders keep feeding rising debt demands? Nowadays, banks lending to US homeowners usually resell that debt to investors in the form of "mortgage-backed securities." Because the US government is believed to guarantee those securities, more or less, investors around the world have been buying them. The two biggest buyers recently have been banks in Japan and the People's Republic of China.

They are therefore—and note the irony—among the biggest ultimate recipients of the monthly mortgage payments made by American homeowners. The US housing bubble postpones bursting only so long as Americans keep borrowing and the major housing lenders, including the Japanese and Chinese banks, keep the cycle of rising home prices and rising home indebtedness rolling.

Nothing guarantees that the lending and borrowing binges will continue. Americans' rising debt levels may frighten them into slowing or ending their borrowing. Countless other possibilities from political shifts to military reverses to cultural changes—including the tougher bankruptcy laws that will take effect on October 17—could likewise reduce Americans' abilities or willingness to borrow. Similarly, all sorts of considerations may dissuade lenders, foreign or domestic, from continuing to provide credit. If and when either the borrowing or the lending slows, the housing bubble will likely burst. As home buying slows, housing prices will stop rising. Inventories of new homes will become difficult to sell, resulting in lower home prices. Housing construction will stop, raising unemployment in that industry and all others dependent on it. Rising unemployment will likely further depress home prices since the unemployed cannot maintain mortgage payments, and so on.

The economic optimism required to keep the Bush regime afloat regularly issues from economists and politicians. They offer reasons why American homeowners will keep borrowing and why lenders will keep providing the credit. Because rising home prices have made American homeowners richer, they are willing to keep borrowing. Likewise, lenders are willing to provide more credit to richer borrowers. Yet these "reasons" explain nothing; they merely describe the bubble itself. Identical predictions in 1999 promised that rising stock prices enriched stock owners who could then afford more stock purchases at higher prices and so on. Yet, the stock market bubble burst. Why should the same not happen to housing prices?

Some optimists try another line of reasoning. Japan and China will keep lending to US homeowners because, if they do not, a collapse in the US housing market will hurt them. Japan and China depend heavily on sales of their goods to Americans. An economic downturn here will cut demand for their goods and so spread to them. Thus, they have no choice but to support the US economy by endless lending to Americans.

This argument's flaw emerges from a brief look at capitalism's history. Every previous capitalist depression, including the devastating one in 1929, was thought to be impossible *because everyone wanted to avoid it since everyone foresaw how a depression would hurt everyone*. Today again, US homeowners, businesses and the government want to avoid a burst housing bubble. The Japanese and Chinese banks and government as well as all the other lenders into the US housing boom want the same. The history of capitalism teaches us that what everyone wants provides no guarantee that it will happen. Everyone may want to keep the boom afloat, but because everyone is also hyper-vigilant to get out of a market that seems to be on the way down, once a downturn starts, it can quickly become a collapse.

It has happened many times. Once again, capitalism brings us to a precipice. Surely the human race can devise a better system. And if not now, when?

US Housing Boom Goes Bust

24 July 2006

A sharp reversal is now hitting the US housing market: another of this system's endemic boom-bust cycles. As is widely known, over the last decade at least, while the US economy became sharply more unequal (rapidly rising gap between rich and poor), it managed to avoid a severe recession. Goods and services purchases kept rising fast enough to keep unemployment from worsening as much as it otherwise would have (given outsourcing, automation, and other factors diminishing the quality and quantity of jobs in America: see Stanley Aronowitz, *Just Around the Corner: The Paradox of the Jobless Recovery*, Philadelphia Temple University Press, 2005).

The remarkable economic reality was that American workers' real wages did not rise across these years. Their stagnant wages would not have allowed those rising consumer purchases. What financed them instead was debt. The US working class took on levels of personal and household debt never before seen in this or any other country. Some of that debt (credit cards) was unsecured by any collateral. But much of that debt was secured by home mortgages. American workers borrowed massive amounts of money at historically low interest rates by increasing their mortgage debts. Thus the US housing market enabled American workers to borrow more, which they used to make the rising purchases that kept the economy from sinking into deep recession or depression.

Basically, it worked like this. People borrowed to buy or expand a home. Housing prices (home values) were bid up. With more value in their now higher-priced homes, American workers had more collateral with which to borrow more. The boom in building and improving homes generated a huge portion of the rising consumer spending that kept the US economy afloat. This cycle of borrowing, building and borrowing more and building more produced an historic run-up in home prices alongside an historic rise in consumer debt. The rapidly increased borrowing allowed all kinds of consumer spending to rise, not only spending on housing. It all worked out very nicely so long as borrowing and spending kept rising and raising each other.

But the building has now stopped growing and started tanking. The *LA Times* reports that the California Realtors Association recently adjusted its projection for total housing sales in 2006 from a fall of 2 percent to a fall instead of 16.8 percent. Hello! Usually, where California goes, so goes the nation. Thus, the chief executive of the largest homebuilding corporation in the US, D.R. Horton, Inc., told investment analysts that his company's national sales "fell off the Richter scale" in June 2006. According to *Money Week* magazine, Ameriquest—a leading US mortgage lending company—recently announced that it is closing 229 branches and laying off 3,500 employees. The mortgage lending business is tanking as housing sales drop.

Drastically fewer new home sales have numerous economic effects. They undermine the building of new homes and thereby reduce employment in the home building businesses and in all the businesses dependent on home building (furniture producers, mortgage lenders, appliance manufactures, landscapers, etc.). Consider, for instance, that California now has an historic 500,000 licensed real estate agents: one for every 55 adults in the state. With fewer homes being sold, these people will compete within a fast shrinking real estate market. Many will be unable to earn an income and forced to accept jobs in other industries at lower pay, thus exerting downward pressure on pay scales generally.

Falling new home sales will force down new home prices. Sellers of older homes will face competition from falling new home prices, so they, too, will lower their prices to find buyers. Falling home prices generally reduce the "home equity" that can function as collateral for mortgage loans. Borrowers will find it harder to get mortgage loans even as they become increasingly anxious about the declining values of the homes they have borrowed against so heavily. Foreclosures are rising nationally as owners cannot maintain payments (since adjustable rate mortgage payments increase with rising interest rates). Thus we face rising unemployment spreading out from declining home building plus reduced mortgage borrowing plus rising mass anxiety about household debt and about falling home values (most Americans' largest single asset—if they have any appreciable assets—are their homes). Under these conditions, the rising tide of purchases of goods and services made possible by the cycle of home building and mortgage borrowing is not only ending, it is reversing at a fast clip.

The housing boom is going bust and will, unless offset by some equally massive economic improvement elsewhere, take the US economy down with it. No such offsetting economic change is now on the horizon. Nor do US leaders show an awareness of the problem or a plausible solution. Bush has nothing to say. Federal Reserve chief Bernanke, according to the LA Times article, told Congress on July 20 that the US housing decline is "orderly." Nor have the utterly compromised Democrats anything much better to offer.

Finally, much of the money lent to US homeowners as their mortgages ballooned came ultimately from Japanese and Chinese lenders. They made such loans as investments of the dollars they had earned from their exports to the US (far larger than their imports from the US). Japan and China—both among the world's four largest economies—will be hurt by any sharp downturn in US consumer spending. They will have to reassess their domestic economic and foreign trade situations. They will further question whether to keep their investments in US dollar mortgages and the US economy generally. They may well dump such US investments in favor of other uses and other places for their money. If so, their decisions will, in turn, have all sorts of further effects on the US including rising interest rates and unemployment.

The American working class is very likely in for rough economic times made more dangerous by their huge personal debt. Social tensions in the US will continue to rise with or without diversions provided by Rove and Bush (Christian fundamentalism at home, unilateral militarized imperialism abroad alone or with "partners" and "coalitions," domestic jingoism, homeland security alarmism, etc.). And still no organized political opposition to channel the riding tension into progressive social change.

What Dream? Americans All *Renters* Now!

13 August 2008

U ntil the early 1980s, homes in the US were mostly owned by the families living in them. By 2008, all that changed. Now US homes are actually owned—about 60 percent of the average home—by mortgage lenders. The families in them own the other 40 percent of the home's value. The average US home "owner" actually owns less of his or her home than the mortgage lenders do. Home "owners" have become more like renters: owning ever less of their homes, they can remain only so long as they pay monthly to the lenders who own ever more.

In the 1960s and 1970s, homes were like investments into which workers poured their fix-it labor, their free time, and what money they could save from their wages. But since the mid-1970s, stagnant real wages for US workers threatened the rising levels of consumption that they had come to expect as their American birthright and the measure of their personal worth and success. To realize the American dream of rising consumption since the 1970s, workers had to borrow. Outstanding mortgage debt went from around $1 trillion in 1980 to over $10 trillion in 2007. Home mortgage debt is the total money borrowed by US homeowners and secured by the lender's right to take the home via "foreclosure" if the owner does not pay the loans back with interest every month. From 1980 to 2007, other forms of consumer credit (especially credit card debt) rose from $300 billion to $2.5 trillion. These were historically unprecedented debt levels.

In the 1960s and 1970s, Americans owned about two thirds of the market values of their homes; those two thirds were their "home equity" while the remaining third was what they owed to mortgage lenders. Then, just when real wages stopped rising, home equity started falling. From the early 1980s to 2006, families borrowed ever more so that their home equity fell as a percentage of the home's value. The fall in the home equity percentage was cushioned then by the fact that home prices rose until 2006. While mortgage borrowing reduced families' home equity, the rising home prices raised home equity. From the early 1980s to 2006, mortgage borrowing simply rose faster than home prices. However, when home prices stopped rising and began the fall that is still underway, the home equity portion of US homes plunged downward, hitting 47.9 percent in the last quarter of 2007.

The end of rising real wages in the US drove workers to keep consuming by using up the only wealth accumulated by the homeowners among them. As they borrowed, they lost their home equity. Now, as stagnant wages, rising unemployment, and rising prices take their tolls, Americans by the millions are losing their homes. Those able to keep their homes have dwindling home equity and consequently dwindling capacity to borrow. All workers will spend less, so stores will sell less, so producing companies will lay off other workers: there's no point in producing what you cannot sell. Laid-off workers will then cut back their spending and reinforce the economic decline. We are in that typical downward spiral that economists eventually call recession or, if it gets bad enough and/or lasts long enough, depression.

And that indeed is where we stand in the summer of 2008 amid the vanishing American dream. But if this prospect is troubling, one way to avoid worrying is to listen to the spokespersons of the US government or indeed most politicians and big business folks: they see a turning point, they are looking up, they seem sure the worst is behind us, they celebrate the greatness of free enterprise, and so on. Fires always seem to bring out fiddlers.

By way of conclusion, consider a speech given by a political leader when the economic crisis was already in full bloom last September. This quotation *today* opens this candidate's website devoted to economic issues:

"I believe that America's free market has been the engine of America's great progress. It's created a prosperity that is the envy of the world. It's led to a standard of living unmatched in history. And it has provided great rewards to the innovators and risk-takers who have made America a beacon for science, and technology, and discovery. . . . We are all in this together. From CEOs to shareholders, from financiers to factory workers, we all have a stake in each other's success because the more Americans prosper, the more America prospers."

—Barack Obama, New York, 17 September 2007

6. Government Intervention in the Economy

Bernanke Expectations: New Fed Chairman, Same Old, Same Old

8 January 2005

The disconnect between Bush regime deed and American public need grows: in Iraq, in New Orleans, on global warming and off-shore oil drilling, from Social Security to selecting Supreme Court Justices, the gulf widens. The choice of Dr. Benjamin S. Bernanke to succeed Alan Greenspan as Federal Reserve Board Chairman follows the pattern.

Just as the ship *Economic* sails into increasingly choppy waters, we will suffer a Princeton professor famous for sublime confidence that all is well in the economy or, if slightly off-course, easily corrected. In this he looks like Alan Greenspan, who managed similar confidence in the crazy stock market bubble of the 1990s (the US, he said then, had wondrously achieved "a new economy"). Greenspan caved to political pressures and waxed optimistic even in the face of policies he had earlier warned against. Similarly, Bernanke began major speeches in March and April of this year with the stunning line: "On most dimensions the U.S. economy appears to be performing well."

Like Greenspan, Bernanke is minimally distressed that US consumers have stopped saving and borrowed beyond anything ever seen before, that the debts owed by the government to foreign institutions and individuals break all records, that the balance of our trade with other countries shows unprecedented levels of deficit, and that the inequalities of wealth and income in the US have widened drastically across recent decades. Unlike the retiring Greenspan, who at least admits that a housing bubble now exists, Bernanke denies even that in his drive to reassure all who will still listen. Bernanke on the US economy replicates Bush, Cheney, and Rumsfeld on the US position in the world.

As the new Fed chairman, Bernanke, a professor of economics, should raise more than eyebrows. His is an academic discipline now extremely disconnected from most people. In the past, economics professors regularly focused on asking big, important questions about capitalist economies—why does cyclical instability plague them, why can't they eradicate poverty, why are some capitalist nations rich and so many others poor, why does the full employment many demand elude them? They also, at least sometimes, faced up to even bigger questions: what are the relative benefits and costs of capitalism versus socialism and communism, and how do economic systems interact with politics and culture in shaping and changing social systems? Students who cared and wanted to make a better world took economics courses to get answers to such questions. But for the last 40 years, economics professors turned away from the big questions and aimed instead to dazzle onlookers with their abstract mathematical methods focused on ever smaller questions. The economics professors wanted the prestige and financial rewards of their colleagues in the natural sciences and engineering departments.

But while top physicists and biologists remained focused on the big issues—matter, energy, and life—and debated fundamentally alternative theories about them, most economists did not. They endlessly repeated celebrations of capitalist market efficiency expressed in ever-greater mathematical and statistical details. The few dissenters too mostly stressed mathematical methods over substance, because method had come to matter far more that substance in economics.

The business community understood this and so turned increasingly away from economics to business schools. There, businesses found a kind of economics worth learning and practically useful. The general population lost interest in abstruse academic economics, while watching with growing disdain as economists said what politicians and big business paid them to say. What remained to the academic economists were three small audiences. The first audience was themselves: economics professors and their graduate students impressed one another with their technical methods, accordingly hired one another, and so further insulated themselves from the rest of the world. The second audience was larger but captive: undergraduates who were taught that the US economy was efficient, fair, and well controlled (by private property, markets, and maybe a little government intervention). The third audience was the nation's political leaders (in business and government) who needed the veneer of "economic analysis" from expert advisors to cover their political decisions about taxes, government spending, economic regulation, and the like. The relatively few who refused to serve these audiences in these ways found themselves either excluded from academic jobs or else given second-class teaching positions.

Bernanke is a product and enthusiastic booster of all that academic economics has become. His career is a paradigm case of serving the first and third of the audiences listed above. His technical economics won the profession's rewards, and by successfully pandering to conservative politicians he has been appointed chief economic cheerleader. His Princeton resume lists many "honors and fellowships," not one of which has anything to do with teaching students. As survivors of most economics courses can readily attest, economics teaching is generally awful.

Yet the Fed has concrete tasks to perform. In addition to controlling the money supply, these tasks include managing (1) the price level of US goods and services (i.e., preventing inflations and deflations), (2) the exchange rate between dollars and other world currencies, (3) interest rates, and (4) international capital flows. The Fed comes under intense and contradictory pressures on all these tasks.

Corporations—the biggest, richest, and most powerful "interest groups"—push in contradictory directions. Some want inflation, others seek deflation; some demand higher interest rates, others want them lower, and so on. Bernanke has, in effect, promised to negotiate these pressures much as Greenspan did. That means he will go with the preponderance of pressures, subject to the control of the Bush Republicans who put him in place (so long as they stay in control).

Thus we can expect loud commitments to prevent inflation. Bernanke will likely continue Greenspan's use of recent strategic changes in government statistics on prices (like shifting among "consumer price indexes," "core indexes," "personal consumption expenditure indexes," or endlessly increasing the number of "seasonal adjustments" to price statistics). Here the point will be to make numbers say what is most convenient for Fed policies. So too Bernanke will raise interest rates "to combat inflation" except, as with Greenspan, when financial bubbles burst and interest rates need to be dropped fast to contain the disaster. We can likewise expect Bernanke assertions about maintaining the value of the dollar except when dangerous US trade imbalances produce enough pressures to "force" us to devalue the dollar.

In short, Bernanke will manage the money supply in the "interests of the US economy"—the preferred euphemism for accommodating the prevailing business pressures—at an extremely precarious, unstable, and dangerous point in America's history. The mess left behind by Greenspan is now Bernanke's. The mandate is the same, the problem greater. The Greenspan Fed generated, denied, spun, and surfed the waves created by a series of bubbles by which illusions of prosperity were maintained. Bernanke will do likewise, but it's harder now.

Nothing illustrates this better than those 2005 speeches (referred to above) where he invented the convenient "global savings glut" theory. Bernanke uses it to absolve top policymakers (Greenspan and Bush) of responsibility for the current world situation in which money desperately needed around the world for economic development is instead loaned to a debt-gorged and earnings-short US economy. These days, Americans buy more from the world (imports) than we sell to them (exports). Since revenues from exports fall short of the costs of the imports, the difference is generated by borrowing from abroad. Likewise, because Bush wages expensive wars while cutting taxes (on the corporations and wealthy households that finance his campaigns), the government runs a deficit. To spend more than it receives in taxes, the government borrows from abroad. Hence, the largest US net debt to the rest of the world in history—now in the scary neighborhood of $2.5 trillion. This huge debt jeopardizes the US dollar as foreigners worry lest its economic problems render the US ever less able to pay them back.

But Bernanke dismisses such accounts of the current world economic mess. Instead, he turns the story around. The problem lies with foreigners—a move as convenient as blaming the "insurgents" for the disaster in Iraq. The "foreigners" have saved money but don't "want" to lend or invest it in their own countries. Instead, they choose to lend this "glut of savings" to America. It's their fault. Bernanke's "foreigners" nicely lumps together corporations, governments, and people as if they were one undifferentiated mass, a common move of professors avoiding anything like a class analysis of economies and their interactions. Bernanke scolds them for hurting their own countries. Nice. He concludes by painting his policy goals as helping others to do better for their own countries by keeping their savings there. Such thin sleights of hand were the hallmark of Greenspan's tenure. Bernanke strives to do as well.

Max Fraad-Wolff assisted in preparing this article.

Federal Reserve Twists and Turns

19 September 2007

The Federal Reserve is led by an inveterate "free market solves all economic problems best" kind of guy. Mr. Bernanke loves Milton Friedman passionately and says so. This is what big business wants to hear when it is making lots of money, when it wants tax reductions to boost profits, and when it wants government deregulation for the same reason. But these days big business, and especially big financial business, wants to hear a different tune. That's because something has gone badly wrong in the free market.

Somehow, normally proper banks, hedge funds, securities dealers, mortgage companies, and the companies that rate the risks associated with what they all do got on the wrong track. They pushed loans on people and businesses who might not be able to pay back, they drew others into sharing those loans, and they were not always clear or honest about the risks involved. So suddenly, when some of those borrowers could no longer pay back the interest or principal they owed, the credit system began to unravel. Lenders became painfully aware that the IOUs they owned were often worth much less than what they had thought. Shocked and awed, they cut back on lending money.

Nowadays, they trust no one. Borrowers—both those who are risky bets and those who aren't—have ever greater trouble getting loans. In a capitalism utterly dependent on massive, intertwined networks of credit, a breakdown in the lender-borrower relation threatens the economy and beyond that the society as a whole.

The free-market, no-government-intervention ideology finds itself in a rough patch. So Mr. Bernanke's Federal Reserve sharply cut interest rates on September 18. Let's be clear here. The government intervened to make money for banks, or more precisely to print and distribute money to banks. The grateful banks were told that their interest cost to get this new government-issue money would henceforth be much cheaper. The government hopes that the banks, flush with this cheap new money, will lend it and so revive the credit system. If they do, that might prevent the financial crisis from becoming a general economic crisis. The government—led by anti-government free-market ideologues—is trying to rescue capitalism from financial free markets that have spun out of control and threaten the whole economy.

More interesting than this revelation of the contradictions between how capitalism works (or doesn't) and its ideologies is to consider what this government *did not do* to address the current problems. Last month saw a quarter of a million home foreclosures in the US. One major contributor to the current financial crisis is the incapacity of homeowners to keep paying their monthly mortgage obligations. Thus one way the government might have helped the situation is by helping these homeowners to make those payments or making the payments for them or lending them the money to make the payments. Not only was none of this done, but there is little chance of anything being done anytime soon for these "distressed" home-owners—estimated to reach over 2 million within a year's time.

Nor is the government even considering, let alone doing anything, about the housing industries. And this despite the obvious fact that the "deregulated" dealings among the builders, financiers, mortgage dealers, and securities industries were central causes of today's economic crisis. Apparently, the government is to be kept away from the "efficiency" of the free market until breakdowns occur. Then, when the government is brought in to "solve" those problems, struggles erupt over who will benefit from the government "bail out" and who will not. It is not difficult to guess who wins in those struggles. The banks are already today's prime beneficiaries of the Federal Reserve's intervention, while the foreclosed watch pitifully from the side-lines and the sidewalks outside their former homes.

In Asia and New Orleans, it was a tsunami and a hurricane that took people's homes. Their capitalist economies and the governments they dominate would not take the necessary and perfectly possible steps to prevent or humanely respond to those disasters. In the US today, no weather event touched off our disaster. Instead we have a financial crisis of capitalism and the particular "policies" of the state it controls that combine to deprive millions of their homes. Whereas in Asia and New Orleans, the homeless saw their former homes physically destroyed, here the homeless will gaze upon their former homes, intact and empty, staring back at them.

In contemporary capitalism, the interdependence of the corporations and the state makes it absurd to look to either one for solutions to the problems their cozy relationship generates. The debates about whether regulated is better or worse than deregulated capitalism, about whether more government inter-vention is better than less, miss the point. Today's basic social problems emerge from the interaction of this kind of economy and this kind of state. More or less of one versus the other guar-antees little or no basic changes and thus little or no basic solutions to this system's problems such as the current financial and housing crises.

As Rome Burned, the Emperor Fiddled

13 February 2008

As global finance's house of cards implodes, Bush and Congress fiddle and Bernanke Feddles. When sub-prime mortgages defaulted, debt-backed securities tanked, and credit everywhere contracted. Business investment then shrank as did consumer spending. Recession now looms in the US, if it is not already here. Worry deepens that it might get very bad and last a long time. A fearful private economy appeals to the state, the very institution it had denounced for useless economic meddling for decades. Leaders of private enterprise and their mouthpieces in the media and academia begin to reverse themselves. Suddenly they want the state—that wasteful, corrupt, and inept intrusion on the efficiency of private enterprise and deregulated ("free") markets—to intervene massively in the economy to fix the mess made by private enterprise.

What they wanted and got from Bush and Bernanke are very limited steps likely to fail. They cannot shake the neoliberal notion—even in today's economic crises—that the best government—even when needed urgently—is the one that does the least possible.

So Bernanke's Fed lowered interest rates for a shell-shocked business community and consumers who are already in debt over their capacities and looking to reduce their debts as they head into bad economic times. Lower interest rates will likely *not* stimulate borrowing and spending (the point of lowering interest rates) the way they did before in far different and better circumstances.

Meanwhile Bush and the Congress are collaborating on a fiscal "stimulus" plan whose major components are the rebate of past tax payments back to businesses and individuals. Once again, businesses will likely *not* rush to invest (spend) the returned taxes for the same reason they have been *reducing* their investments over recent months: namely, that the prospects for making profits are now somewhere between poor and non-existent. If businesses don't spend their returned taxes on more goods and services, more *won't* be produced, so more people *won't* be hired, and the current economic downturn will *not* be reversed.

Consumers reeling under unmanageable debts are also more likely than ever to use rebated taxes to reduce their debts. A recent Associated Press-Ipos poll asked what Americans planned to do with tax rebates: 45 percent said they would repay debts; 32 percent would save or invest it in securities, and only 19 percent planned to spend it on goods and services. Those few consumers who do spend tax rebates on goods will, more than ever before, spend them on *imported* consumer goods. Thus what increased consumer spending occurs will disproportionately stimulate not the US but rather the Chinese economy as well as the economies of other sources of US consumer goods imports.

So the picture emerging has the US economy's private sector arranging for the government to make a minimalist, hesitant intervention. Partly this is driven by the wounded but still alive neoliberal consensus against government interventions in the "free market." The hope is that such little steps will, somehow, magically be enough, so that the unwanted reliance on much more massive state intervention will not be required.

What might such heavier intervention look like? The state could do the spending itself—say on housing, schools, daycare centers, health facilities, etc. That is, instead of returning taxes to businesses and people who might well not spend that money or spend it on importing other economies' outputs, the government could do the spending directly and on goods and services produced here. The state might also go into production itself, hiring workers and buying the tools, equipment, and raw materials needed for that production. This would generate income for workers and businesses as well as produce socially needed outputs of products now in short supply (housing for the homeless, good new schools, clinics, etc.). By doing this, the state would no longer leave business investment up to private enterprises' "free choice." The businesses' "freedom" to not invest yielded unacceptable social consequences (deepening recession). In effect, the state would tell private business: you made this mess, so now either you invest enough to correct it or else we the government will replace or supplement private with public investment.

All these steps—and more—have been taken before in American history on other occasions when free, private enterprise produced disastrous economic downturns. Roosevelt's New Deal was forced on him by Americans no longer willing to wait as his government's hesitant, too-little and too-late steps proved inadequate to reverse the Great Depression early in the 1930s. In 2008, the failures of Bush and Bernanke will focus the outrage of Americans on whoever arrives next, McCain, Clinton, or Obama.

Of course, this time history need not and likely will not repeat itself. Many Americans have understood what went wrong with the New Deal. All its achievements (Social Security, state regulation of private industry, public works and public employment, unemployment insurance, etc.) always stopped short of taking away from private corporations' boards of directors their control and use of profits. Those boards thus used the profits across recent decades first to evade and then to attack, weaken, and eventually overthrow most of what the New Deal accomplished.

So this time, massive state intervention may well expand to prevent corporate boards of directors from again using profits to undermine the government's regulations and interventions. Either the state itself may undertake that expansion, or the workers in each enterprise may demand control over profits that, after all, their labor generated. Imagine that: workers insisting that since their jobs, communities, and families depend on what corporations do with profits and since their labor produces those profits, they want half the seats on every enterprise's board of directors to go to democratically elected workers. That, they say, will make sure profits are used for the benefit of everyone dependent on the corporation: not just the managers, directors, and shareholders, but also the workers who are, after all, the majority. Imagine that.

Policies to "Avoid" Economic Crises

6 November 2008

Recently, economist Joseph Stiglitz called the current crisis "avoidable." He blamed it on "ideology, special-interest pressure, populist politics, and sheer incompetence." In tune with the norms of his profession, he proposed "policies" to fix the problem. Debates over the worsening economic crisis increasingly turn on which "policies" to use to stop, reverse, and "avoid" crises. Conservatives and liberals again rehash their old debates over their different policies as McCain and Obama did. The crisis will deepen some more, and then a compromise policy will emerge from the new President and Congress aimed to "solve the problem." Instead, we ought to question the very idea of policy; that questioning would be a real change from past practice.

The problem is this: today's economic crisis was caused by an immense accumulation of factors, far too many for any policy to manage. Here is a partial list. Workers' wages stopped rising since the 1970s; thereafter, they accepted rising loans instead of rising wages as compensation for their greater work and productivity. Corporate profits exploded because they got ever more output per worker (via computerization, etc.) while not paying their workers any more. Corporations deposited their rising profits in banks who then loaned part of them back to workers, another part to investors for stock and then real estate speculations, and yet another part to businesses for mergers. Other factors included low taxes, expensive wars, and resulting US government deficits. Then, too, China's industrialization flooded the US with inexpensive products as that country accumulated our massive dollar payments for them. China then lent those dollars back into the US to finance the government's deficit and further increase banks' loanable funds. All these very different factors helped build up the house of credit that has now crashed the entire economy.

Still other factors also shaped the crisis. New mortgage brokerage practices and credit-card promotions induced more debt than borrowers could afford. Competition among rating companies yielded incorrect assessments of financial risks of trillions in newly invented financial instruments (derivatives). This led to staggering global misallocations of scarce resources. Homebuilders' competition yielded excess construction. The Federal Reserve increased the money supply and lowered interest rates to offset the dot-com bubble burst in 2000.

Nor is this list of factors even nearly complete. No policy emerging from deals between conservative and liberal legislators beset by armies of lobbyists could ever begin to control or manage the immense diversity of the causes of the current crisis. Indeed, no policy of any kind—whether imposed by a dictator, produced by democratic consensus, or anything in between—can "fix the problem." No policy ever did. There are just far too many causes of crises that one can see and list—and too many more not yet seen.

The whole idea of policy is bizarre. The "right policy" represents an absurd claim that this or that law or regulation can somehow undo the many different factors that cumulatively produced this crisis. Policies are "magic potions" offered to populations urgently demanding solutions to real problems. Whether cynically advocated for ulterior motives or actually believed by the politicians, promoters, and professors themselves, policy is the secular cousin of religion.

These days, the conservative policy amounts, as usual, to "let the private economy solve the problems" and "minimize state intervention because it only makes matters worse." Conservatives protect the freedoms of private enterprise, market transactions, and the wealthy from state regulations and controls and from taxes. The liberals' policy, also as usual, wants the state to limit corporate behavior, control and shape market transactions, and tilt the tax system more toward benefiting middle and lower income groups.

Both policies can no more overcome this economic crisis than they overcame past crises. Historically, both conservative and liberal policies fail at least as often as they succeed. Which outcome happens depends on all the factors shaping them and not on the policy a government pursues. Yet, both sides endlessly claim otherwise in desperate efforts at self-justification. Each side trots out its basic philosophy—dressed up as "a policy to achieve solutions." Conservatives and liberals keep debating. Today's crisis simply provides an urgent sort of context for the old debate to continue. Each side hopes to win converts by suggesting that its approach will "solve the economic crisis" while the other's approach will make it worse. Thus the liberals displaced the conservatives in the depths of the Great Depression, the reverse happened in the recession of the 1970s, and the liberals may now regain dominance. In no instance were adopted policies successful in solving the crises in any enduring way. The unevenness and instability of capitalism as a system soon brought another crisis crashing down on our economy and society.

The basic conservative message holds that the current economic crisis is NOT connected to the underlying economic system. The crisis does NOT emerge from the structure of the corporate system of production. It is NOT connected to the fact that corporate boards of directors, responsible to the minority that owns most of their shares, make all the key economic decisions while the enterprise's employees and the vast majority of the citizenry have to live with the consequences. The very undemocratic nature of the capitalist system of production is NOT related to crisis in the conservative view. The basic liberal message likewise disconnects today's crisis from the capitalist production system. Rather, each side insists that all crises would have been and would now be "avoidable" if only the right policy were in place.

Conservatives and liberals share more than a careful avoidance of connecting the crisis to the underlying capitalist system. They are also complicit in blocking those who do argue for that connection from making their case in politics, the media, or the schools. While conservative and liberal policies do little to solve crises, the debate between them has largely succeeded in excluding anti-capitalist analyses of economic crises from public discussion. Perhaps that exclusion—rather than solving crises—is the function of those endlessly rehashed policy debates between liberals and conservatives.

Lotteries: Disguised Tax Injustice

2 February 2009

Lotteries, now run by most of our 50 states, are disguised forms of taxation that fall most heavily on those least able to pay. In today's economic crisis, state leaders face rising resistance to taxation from everyone. Therefore, many of them plan to expand lotteries even more, hoping that no one realizes they represent a kind of masked tax. In the elegant words of conservative South Carolina State Senator Robert Ford, reported by the Associated Press, "Gambling ain't no blight on society." To fight them, we need first to expose state lotteries as disguised and very unfair taxation.

The rising importance of state lottery revenues is reflected in the basic statistics. In 1998, states' gambling revenues were $14.9 billion; by 2007 the number had grown to $23.3 billion. Most of that money comes from lotteries, though revenue from casinos is also rising. Both Republicans and Democrats have been moving steadily toward ever more lottery sales; there is no reason to doubt that they will continue.

Where do lottery revenues come from? A famous recent study by Cornell University researchers reached these conclusions:

> [L]otteries are extremely popular, particularly among low income citizens.... [I]ndividuals with lower incomes substitute lottery play for other entertainment.... [L]ow income consumers may view lotteries as a convenient and otherwise rare opportunity for radically improving their standard of living.... [T]he desperate may turn to lotteries in an effort to escape hardship. We... find a strong and positive relationship between sales and poverty rates....

In another study, Duke University researchers in 1999 found that the more education one has *the less* one spends on lottery tickets: dropouts averaged $700 annually compared to college graduate's $178; and that those from households with annual incomes below $25,000 spent an average of nearly $600 per year on lottery tickets, while those from households earning over $100,000 averaged $289; blacks spent an average of $998, while whites spent $210.

Put simply, lotteries take the most from those who can least afford them. Thus, still another study of state lotteries concluded: "We find that the implicit tax is regressive in virtu-ally all cases." Instead of taxing those most able to pay, state leaders use lotteries to disguise a regressive tax that targets the middle and even more the poor. Just as the richest were getting much richer from 2001 to 2006, the middle and poor were getting ever more heavily taxed by means of lotteries.

How do states use their lottery revenues? Some 50 to 70 percent go to the winners; 20 to 40 percent go to pay for states' public services (often education); and the rest (10 to 20 percent) go for the "expenses" of running lotteries. In 2006, over half of California's lottery receipts used for these "expenses" were paid as commissions to retailers for selling lottery tickets. Sales per retail outlet in 2006 averaged $188,000 in California (and $405,000 in New York). For many retailers across the country, profits from the fully automated selling of lottery tickets significantly boost their bottom lines.

Lotteries actually redistribute wealth from the poorer to the richer. The vast majority of middle-income and poor people buy tickets and win nothing or nearly nothing, while a tiny number of winners become wealthy. Lotteries raise ever more money for states from their middle-income and poor citizens *rather than* those most able to pay, thereby allowing the rich to escape rising taxes. Retail merchants get state welfare in profitable commis-sions on lottery sales. Politicians boast that they "did not raise taxes"—having raised money instead by lottery ticket sales.

The effects of lotteries in today's economic crisis are even more perverse. Lotteries take huge sums from masses of people who would otherwise likely have spent that money on goods and services whose production gave people jobs. The lotteries then distribute over half that money to a few, suddenly enriched, individuals who likely will *not* spend as much (and thus generate *fewer* jobs). This is the exact opposite of the kind of economic stimulus a depressed economy needs. Yet many states are now planning increases in lottery sales to raise money "in these bad times."

Lotteries are also powerful ideological and political weapons. They reinforce notions that individual acts—buying lottery tickets—are appropriate responses to society's economic problems. Lotteries help to distract people from collective action to solve the economic crisis by changing society. Lotteries' massive advertising shows an audacity of hype: shifting people from hope for the social fruits of collective action to hope for the personal fruits of individual gambling.

Finally, compare lotteries (disguised taxes) with taxes not wearing masks. Taxes raise money that mostly goes to fund states' provision of public services. Lottery revenues make a few winners wealthy at the expense of the mass of taxpayers; only small portions of lottery revenues fund states' services. We can socially target taxes to tap those most able to pay; we cannot do that with lotteries. Taxes can enable the states to provide public education, child and elderly care, public transportation and so on *without using state employees to push us to gamble more*, which is what lotteries do.

The issue here is not gambling per se; the point is not to engage the religious, moral, or mental health debates over gambling. Rather, what matters is the cynical use of state lotteries to disguise unfair tax burdens even as they worsen the economic crisis.

As an alternative to lottery expansions, states could together pass a property tax levied on property in the form of stocks and bonds (see elsewhere in this volume: "Evading Taxes, Legally"). Let's recall that many states already tax property in the form of land, homes, commercial and industrial buildings, automobiles, and business inventories. There is no justification for excluding stocks and bonds from the property tax; *stocks and bonds are the form in which the richest among us hold most of their property*. A property tax on stocks and bonds could raise far more than lotteries do, it would tax those most able to pay, and it would end the injustice of allowing owners of stocks and bonds to avoid the taxes now levied on the other sorts of property most Americans own (cars, homes, etc.).

7. International Dimensions of the Crisis

Immigration and Class

10 May 2006

Migration between countries occurs if and when it "resolves" social and especially class contradictions inside both of them. One set of contradictions pushes people out of a country just as another set of contradictions in other countries pulls them in. Finally, while migration "resolves" some social contradictions, it likewise engenders or aggravates others.

These days, capitalist globalization (e.g., US multinationals producing exports in China) dumps cheap goods into countries whose domestic producers cannot compete with them. It introduces global retail trading corporations (e.g., Wal-Mart) that destroy domestic merchants. Finally, globalization's ups and downs produce sudden inflows and outflows of private capital that further destabilize national economies. In these ways, capitalist globalization exacerbates social contradictions. Migration follows as a way people and corporations try to cope with those contradictions.

In many less developed economies, their two main domestic class structures have been under extreme and rising pressure for some years. Small self-employed producers cannot generate enough value from what they produce and sell to secure their enterprises' reproduction. Domestic capitalist enterprises are rarely capable of competing with multinational corporations as the latter invade their markets, compete for inputs of raw materials, tools, and equipment, and squeeze their access to credit. The capitalist class structures—the invading multinationals and the surviving domestic capitalists—rarely generate enough new jobs to absorb the masses rendered unemployed by the multinational invasion. As desperate farmers migrate to the urban and industrial areas internally, they not only swell the already high unemployment there; they also quickly discover the two possible "solutions" for that unemployment.

One group's solution is to enter the vast, poor, and insecure "informal sector" (an unstable mix of the legal and illegal small-scale producers of very low-price and low-profit goods and services). The customs of that overcrowded sector often differ radically from everything this group knew and believed before their class structures were dissolved by or subordinated to the invading multinationals. Across the globe, the masses are traumatized on a vast scale through their passage into the informal sectors. Long-standing conventions of work, dress, family life, sexual activity, kinship, religious activity, and so on break down quickly and thoroughly. Another group's solution is emigration—either instead of entry into the informal sector or after experiencing it.

It is important to note that it is not poverty that produces emigration. Poverty has been the norm in many parts of the world for long periods of time without provoking emigration. Emigration is usually a result of the interaction of external and internal conditions dissolving deep structures of production and patterns of social life generally. Recent waves of emigration are no exception. The catalyst was the dissolution of the class structures of the self-employed and the smaller capitalist producers in the Third World. Indeed, the few Third World capitalists who prospered—usually by finding ways to serve and thereby survive the multinationals' invasions—also supported (overtly or covertly) mass emigration. Their societies were polarizing into a "modern" sector (the relatively few successful capitalists and their hangers-on among the professionals, state officials and workers, upscale retailers, and various personal service providers) and that "informal" sector. The political problem everywhere was and remains how to manage and contain the potential explosion of masses of traumatized internal migrants living in extremely precarious conditions. They represented a frightening specter of potential political opposition to the local "modernizing" classes. How much better to have them leave and perhaps send back money to desperate relatives left behind!

The prospect of mass emigration struck the modernizers as the best available solution to the problem of their "informal sectors." They did not want to undertake (much less pay for) mass work programs financed, say, by taxes on domestic and multinational capitalists or domestic redistributions of wealth and income. They did not dare take any domestic steps that risked the enmity of the multinational "bloc" comprising corporations and the international agencies they or their home governments controlled. Such enmity could lead to capital outflows, currency collapses, and the social unrest thereby further provoked. Nor did they imagine the possibility of confronting the multinational bloc through coordination of multiple Third World economies (such as one that is struggling to be born now in Latin America). Thus, leaders of many Third World governments, together with their corporate supporters, found ways to facilitate mass emigration.

At the same time, globalization's other side—the rich industrial capitalist economies (RICEs)—has also been experiencing class contradictions and crises. Global competition drives all capitalists in the RICEs aggressively to lower commodity prices without reducing profits. One key means to this end entails moving jobs to cheaper workers overseas (outsourcing, capital exports, etc.). Another involves moving cheaper workers, via immigration, into jobs inside the RICEs. Thus, such US industries as agriculture, construction, tourism, restaurants and hotels, and hospitals—all industries that cannot readily outsource—have long recruited and supported the immigration of low-wage workers, legally or illegally. Immigration "solves" their competitive problems.

However, solving one problem provokes another. Mass immigration of low-wage workers has all sorts of contradictory effects on the host society. The resources available to (especially local) governments and the demands on public services change, often in ways provoking conflicts between new immigrants and their non-immigrant neighbors. Conflicts also result as immigrants raise and lower various wage and price levels, shift housing patterns and conditions, increase profits for some enterprises while diminishing those of others, change party memberships and politics, and alter the mix of religious institutions and practices where they settle.

US corporate recruiters and employers of immigrants bear no responsibility to finance and thereby ease their integration into local communities. The burden thus falls on the government at a time, especially in the US, when state resources are already stretched and objects of significant social conflict. Immigrants and immigration get caught up in aggravated domestic conflicts, often as scapegoats in a nation with a long history of displacing class conflicts onto anti-immigrant agitation as well as inter-racial, inter-ethnic, and inter-religious tensions. Immigrants today, like those before them, suffer all sorts of discriminations.

Today as in the past, the issue is political. Will immigrants and non-immigrants seek to solve their economic and social problems by battling each other or will they unite to seek other solutions? Will domestic social policies in their new countries provide all immigrants as well as natives with jobs, homes, and schools of quality to facilitate their integration while minimizing discriminations against them? Will those domestic policies be financed by funds drawn chiefly from the corporate profits fattened by cheap immigrant labor? Will foreign policies of leading nations require the immigrants' countries of origin to provide decent economic options for their people so that emigration becomes a genuine choice rather than a desperate last resort? It is difficult to see such changes emerging so long as the class structures and imperatives of capitalism remain hegemonic in the economies at both ends of the migrants' journey.

What the immigrants and the natives thus need most—and what might therefore be a basis for strategic unity—is a change in the class structures at both ends of the migration process. To say that such a strategy is not "realistic" neglects the fact that 200 years of capitalism as the hegemonic class structure and countless "realistic immigration reforms" have not fundamentally altered modern migration. It remains the scene of mass suffering, social and personal trauma, grotesque injustice, and painful struggles pitting immigrants against non-immigrants while migration's capitalist beneficiaries keep profiting from it.

Global Oil Market Dangers

12 July 2006

International intrigues and eventually war—with all its now daily horrors—flow partly from the highly unstable economics of global oil. Not only has this been true for a long time, it promises to continue that way unless and until some mass movement ends it. The report of US planning to bomb Iran (see Seymour Hersh's *New Yorker* 10 July 2006 article) is only the latest in a long history worth revisiting for the lessons it teaches.

Across the last century, as every country became increasingly dependent on oil, profits from exploring, producing, transporting, and refining it attracted business attention. Competition among these businesses eventuated, as usual, in the losers being gobbled up by the winners. A few international oil giants arrived at an especially powerful—although not unchallenged—position in the global oil market. They have tried ever since to manipulate and control, as far as possible, the price of the oil they sell.

They did this partly by strategic locations and timing of their huge investments in exploration, production, transport, and refining. Sometimes, they coordinated investments and operations among themselves to gain monopoly benefits. They pressured and often bribed political leaders to make decisions favoring oil profiteering. While they have done exceedingly well, they could never entirely control the oil market. Too many other players wielded influence. Hence that market's extreme instability.

Businesses who had to buy oil to keep production running resented and fought high oil prices. Workers who drive from home to job to shopping and who heat their homes with oil sometimes mounted backlashes to high oil prices. Smaller companies, drawn by oil profits, entered and wedged into the oil market. Nationalism in oil-rich nations led their leaders to gain some control—often via mass movements—of their oil. Those leaders then added their market manipulations to those of the giant oil corporations. Other countries sought to escape their costly dependence on the international oil market for their oil imports. They cut deals that sometimes undermined cozy arrangements among the oil giants and the oil-rich countries. Many sought and some found new oil sources, which further destabilized the oil market. Nor was oil immune to the larger social changes over the last century: the recessions, depressions, and inflations; the political revolutions; the rise of the motor vehicle and plastics industries; the mass population movements, the environmental shifts, and so on.

The result was a chaotic volatility of oil prices within a market always manipulated—more or less successfully—by giant corporations and national leaders alternatively cooperating, competing, or doing both at once. Rising oil prices constrained or destroyed countless efforts at economic, political, and cultural developments across the globe. Falling prices likewise influenced modern history. But most of all, the instability imposed huge costs and global inefficiencies that disrupted and distorted economic development for the world's majority. Thus, global inequalities grew across the century with oil's importance.

Consider this brief modern history of the oil market's wild gyrations. Between 1947 and 1973, oil prices experienced multiple 20–30 percent oscillations. These were caused chiefly by the Korean War, Mossadegh's effort to nationalize Iranian oil, Eisenhower's imposition of Import Quotas and then their removal in 1971, the late 1950s recession, and the Vietnam War. From 1973 to 1981, oil prices tripled—with smaller oscillations along the way—as the Arab embargo responded to the Yom Kippur War, OPEC acquired the ability to control supplies, the Iranian revolution deposed the Shah, and Iraq went to war against Iran. Beyond these major shapers of oil prices, secondary factors in these years included the opening of North Sea and Alaskan oil sources and President Carter's phase-out of US oil price controls. From 1981 to 1998, the world oil price collapsed, again with minor oscillations en route, from roughly $65 to $13 per barrel. Adjusting these oil prices to constant 2004 dollars makes no significant difference: the oil price collapse was very real. Crucial to the collapse was the end of the Iran–Iraq war and OPEC supply increases.

Since 1998, it has been OPEC supply shifts (partly shaped by political crises and governmental shifts inside OPEC member states), the massive Russian exports of oil, the oil-absorbing economic booms in China and India, and the US invasion of Iraq (and now also the menacing of Iran) that have combined to first lower (by over 50 percent) and then triple world oil prices.

Oil companies—already huge but increasingly integrated, merged, and global across the post-war period—were influential in shaping all of the above political decisions. Their investment strategies aimed both to take advantage of the wild oil price upswings and to protect themselves against the downswings. Not least among their strategies was widespread dissemination of arguments picturing the oil companies as merely passive responders to the "free" market and hence without substantial responsibility for that market's volatility. Oil-friendly politicians remain key to repeating such arguments, while elaborating them "scientifically" is assigned to "free-market" economists.

The wild volatility of oil prices has had enormous, history-changing social effects and costs. For example, across Putin's presidency in Russia, its oil exports rose from $14 billion to $127 billion. These export revenues helped to offset (for a few Russians) the economic collapse that has afflicted Russia since 1989. Little mystery surrounds Putin's domestic policy (keep state controls over Russia's energy industry) or his foreign policy priority (secure and expand foreign oil and gas markets). Russia's dealings in Central Asia and the Ukraine, its rapprochement with China, and the increasingly tense relations with the US follow.

To take another example, in the 1970s, the US relied on imports for 33 percent of its oil consumption; today that number has nearly doubled. The US government's commitment to "oil independence" is at best a reality far in the future. Nearly 75 percent of US oil imports come from five countries: Canada, Mexico, Saudi Arabia, Venezuela, and Nigeria. The connection of oil interests to NAFTA, the US alliance with Saudi Arabia (9/11 notwithstanding), attempts to overthrow Chavez, policies toward the civil wars in Nigeria, and the intense "US concern" about Mexico's recent presidential election is an analytical no-brainer.

Deepening global oil dependence interwoven with extreme oil price volatility continues to shape world history in basic and dangerous ways. Competition to make the most from oil price rises and to protect the most against their declines produces or aggravates serious domestic conflicts (e.g., inside Venezuela, Nigeria, Indonesia, and so on). Internationally, the current rapid decline in US–Russian relations, a dangerous global competition between China and the US over oil resources, and a US occupation of Iraq (the world's second largest source of oil) are only some examples.

Because global efforts at reducing oil dependency via production of alternative energy sources or reduction of energy usage are inadequate, oil will continue be a crucially important world commodity. The current organization of the oil market guarantees continued price volatility. Economic, political, and military conflicts inside and between nations proliferate as everyone struggles to cope with the oil market's instabilities.

However, not all oil market players wield equal influence. Huge profits enable the oil giants and some governments to manipulate markets at others' expense. The oil market's instability has not (yet) mobilized those it damages and endangers. Each business, country, and indeed each person struggles for individual solutions to (escapes from) the oil market's effects. Yet social problems—and that is what the unstable oil market surely is—require social solutions. Unless the diverse victims of the oil market's profiteering and instability move, together, to impose such social solutions, their victimization will continue.

China Shapes/Shakes World's Economies

4 September 2006

Over at least the last decade, employers in the West have been able to enlarge profits dramatically by taking simultaneous advantage of the following three opportunities: raising workers' productivity (computerization, etc.), merging to reduce costs (vertical and horizontal), and keeping wages from rising much or at all (outsourcing jobs and importing ever-cheaper consumer imports from China). Under those conditions, profit increases did not require price increases.

But current challenges to China's economic growth now threaten to change those conditions. China faces rising costs for input raw materials including energy, rising wage demands of workers becoming used to industrial employment, and pressures to raise the exchange value of the Chinese currency. Producers of China's exports—most of which are western enterprises with Chinese subsidiaries or partners—have therefore begun to raise their prices. To take one of countless straws in the wind, an August 15 press release from the Xinhua News Agency reports that the majority of the 81 surveyed Chinese producers of automobile brake parts for export plan 5–10 percent price increases over the coming year.

Especially in the United States but also globally, Chinese exports of consumer goods (clothing, toys, appliances, and components for countless other goods) have been a crucial offset to stagnant wages. Employers could keep money wages from rising very much or even falling because workers could buy more of the ever cheaper imports from China. Of course, this practice depends on an absence of challenges to growing gaps between wages and profits. Political tensions and economic inequalities have not emerged to stop this process.

If China-based export producers raise prices to secure profits, then the buyers of Chinese products will have to pay more. Firms will face rising input costs and possible increases in wage demands. No longer will their stagnant money wages be offset by falling Chinese import prices. Likewise, western companies buying Chinese exports as productive inputs will pass through their higher input costs by raising their prices. That too will pressure employees to seek higher wages. This will especially affect the US where already enormous levels of personal debt and a declining real estate market leave most consumers unwilling or unable to respond to rising consumer goods prices with more borrowing.

As Chinese wage rates drift up in local and appreciated currency terms, the advantages of outsourcing to China decline. Western employers will likely become somewhat less tempted to respond to their employees' demands for wage increases by outsourcing. While other low wage producers may gain some momentum, macro price effects are likely to develop. Shifting outsourcing and production from China to India, elsewhere in Asia, etc., would be costly in itself. Moreover, since those regions face the same upward price pressures as China, the problem represented by rising Chinese wages and export prices is unlikely to disappear anytime soon.

Of course, western employers, flush from record profits over the last decade, could decide to absorb the rising prices of what are still relatively cheap imports from China and to absorb rising wages of what are still inexpensive Chinese employees. Then they might not raise their prices. In other words, there is no mechanical necessity of an international inflationary spiral simply because the foreign and domestic enterprises in China are raising their prices. If prices don't rise, however, profits will likely come under enormous pressure.

The contemporary political and cultural dominance of business in general alongside continuing conglomeration suggests that employers may successfully resist strategies that return them to profit levels of earlier years. They will then absorb neither rising prices of their inputs nor rising wages. Instead, they will raise their prices and thereby engage in the gamble of self-reinforcing price-wage spirals. Once launched, these spirals pit the abilities of business to raise prices against the abilities of workers to raise wages. Whoever raises further sooner wins. Indeed, inflationary economies can be times of sharp profit increases too.

What might derail the brewing inflation spiral are not the tepid inconsistencies of a hesitant Federal Reserve. Rather, the serious problems of the US economy—the effects of its fast deflating housing bubble and its dependency on huge capital imports—could draw the global economy into a serious general slowing or decline. Then all bets are off as the downward spiral of competitive dumping contradicts the inflationary scenario.

The stark conclusion here is that the world economy is now functioning on a knife edge. On one side, it risks a rapid fall into an inflationary spiral. On the other side lies descent into recession or worse. No real coordination of development to prevent either disaster occurs. Rather, each enterprise and country plots strategies mixing self-advancement and self-protection. This does not suggest a happy outcome to knife-edge conditions.

Understandably, in such circumstances, some will rediscover the comforting idea that each enterprise pursuing its own self-interest will somehow guarantee an optimum outcome. Others will equally predictably reassure themselves that institutions like the Federal Reserve, OECD, G8, etc. will recognize the problems and implement appropriate solutions. However, realists will redouble their efforts to watch developments henceforth with close attention and rising anxiety, hoping at least to minimize the damage when economies on knife edges tumble and when spirals spin out of control.

Globalization's Risks and Costs

22 October 2006

C ritics have exposed how globalization's benefits have been unequally distributed around the world. Many of the world's poorer regions have become poorer still in relation to the regions that gained. And within regions, it turns out that globalization often worsens wealth and income inequalities. However, critics admit and defenders boast that at least for some—for example, the US—globalization has meant higher wealth, income, or consumption levels. But a closer look raises questions about these beneficiaries of globalization.

The fact is that those who have gained wealth, income, or consumption include many—and likely most—who paid and continue to pay for those gains by absorbing much greater levels of risk. A riskier economy today affects capital and labor now and for years to come. Individuals and businesses behave differently when confronted with more rather than less risk. Greater risks shape the world economy as much, albeit in different ways, as do rising world trade, expanding global capital movements, and spreading multinational corporations. To explore this point, let's briefly consider rising economic risk in the US, a nation widely thought to have benefited from a globalization that its corporations and its government have done much to shape.

Among individuals, the catalog of rising risks is extraordinary. The data on employers shifting ever more from permanent to temporary workers, coupled with the long-term decline of union membership (and hence of workers covered by multi-year contracts), document changes that increase job insecurity. The outsourcing debates reflected and amplified rising anxieties about job security. Consider the testimony of Princeton economics professor Alan Blinder before a US Senate committee on September 23, 2005: "the share of American jobs that is vulnerable to off-shoring is certain to rise... tens of millions of *additional* American workers will start to experience an element of job insecurity..." (the italics are Blinder's).[1]

The dramatic and continuing reduction of private pensions raises the risks of aging for private-sector workers. The rising assaults on Social Security, albeit not yet successful, indicate more danger that its support may be reduced. The number of Americans without health insurance keeps rising. The rising level of personal indebtedness, along with the growing proportion of disposable income required to service personal debts, adds significantly to the uncertainties impinging on current US households. The rapidly growing proportion of homes financed with adjustable-rate, interest-only, and reverse mortgages places household living standards under the constant threat of interest rate increases.

Jacob S. Hacker's recent book, *The Great Risk Shift*, is but the latest in a growing mountain of books and articles that document how the individual lives of Americans have become more economically precarious. Most of these works also show how efforts to cope with rising economic risks have damaged their physical and mental health, personal relationships, and thus quality of life generally. Unfortunately, relatively few publications link the broad scope of rising economic risks to globalization (Hacker's book is especially poor on just that connection). At best they recognize only very limited connections such as outsourcing (as in Blinder's testimony).

On the side of capital, riskiness has also grown. Corporations everywhere confront possibilities of technical improvements by actual or potential competitors anywhere in the world, new or changed laws in foreign countries, new or changed administrative policies there, altered labor market conditions, court decisions in overseas jurisdictions, and so on. Such alterations in the global economy threaten to compromise a US corporation's market here, its raw material source there, patent protection, a foreign direct investment's profitability, and so on.

It takes no special economic expertise to understand that all corporate investment decisions must take these risks into account—or try to—since the success of all investments has become riskier in a globalized environment. Most US corporations cannot effectively monitor all these risks nor rely on the mushrooming consultant enterprises who offer to provide such monitoring for fat fees (themselves costs flowing from the risks). So US corporations have taken other and much costlier steps to cope with those risks.

One index is the amount of money US corporations feel the need to hold on to (rather than invest in growing their enterprise, hiring more employees, etc.). The numbers here are rather stark. Back in 1980, for most US corporations, the ratio of cash holdings as a portion of their total assets was just over 10 percent. By 1995, this ratio had risen to 17 percent, and by 2004 it had risen further to 24 percent. The data are nicely presented in a revealingly titled September 2006 working paper at the National Bureau of Economic Research: "Why Do US Firms Hold So Much More Cash Than They Used To?"[2] The authors conclude that rising economic risks explain the increasing corporate cash hoarding. While they do not explore such hoarding's economic costs, a brief list of such costs would include less employment, lower economic growth, and reduced tax receipts in the US. The secondary and tertiary costs, economic and social, ramifying from rising corporate cash hoarding are too many, too diverse, and too long-lasting to enable any precise measurement.

The conclusion follows rather straightforwardly. To date, most discussions of the distribution of winners and losers from globalization have concentrated on whose wealth, income, or consumption rose and whose fell, relatively and absolutely. However, an overall assessment needs to consider how globalization has imposed rising economic risks and their consequent costs not only on its losers but also and especially on its winners. No one can seriously claim to know, let alone measure, all the gains and costs of globalization, direct and indirect, present and future. However, it is a safe bet that one key foundation for rising skepticism about and opposition to globalization is the growth of economic risks it has spawned even among its beneficiaries.

1 "Inequality and Insecurity," Statement of Alan S. Blinder to JEC/DPC Forum, 23 September 2005 (http://jec.senate.gov/democrats/Documents/Hearings/blindertestimony23sep2005.pdf).
2 Thomas W. Bates, Kathleen M. Kahle, and Rene M. Stulz, September 2006 (http://www.nber.org/papers/w12534).

Foreign Threat to American Business?

12 September 2007

Foreign countries are awash in dollars because they sell so much more to the US than they buy. Increasingly, their governments use some of those dollars to establish and operate investment funds. The funds buy shares in companies around the world. Sometimes they buy companies directly. Called "sovereign investment funds," the IMF estimates that they now possess over $1.5 trillion. New York's Morgan Stanley Bank estimates that could grow to $17.5 trillion in 10 years.

Predictably, some US businesses and their political friends are complaining that foreign governments might—perish the thought—use their sovereign funds to directly control American enterprises and wield political influence. Lawrence Summers, former Treasury secretary and Harvard president, feels that it is appropriate for sovereign funds to buy shares in mutual funds, but "if they make more direct investments, they become meaningful actors in the economy, and that raises many more questions." Summers was quoted in a *New York Times* article (21 August 2007: C1) whose title worried that foreign governments will use these funds to "meddle in US affairs." And all this at a time when the US mix of private mortgage finance and government regulation (or its lack) are exporting financial crises and credit crunch around the globe.

To understand what's going on here, follow the bouncing financial ball. First, we take one prominent example of a country building up a large supply of U$D. The UAE sells oil, pearls, metals, and other goods to the US and world. Oil sales are priced in U$D and this results in their accumulation of a large supply of dollars. The UAE imports little from America. Persistent balance of payment surplus running into tens of billions of dollars leaves them with vast hordes of U$D. The excess dollars accumulate at the UAE central bank (its counterpart to the US Federal Reserve) or in other UAE government bodies.

For a long time, the UAE lent much of that money to the US government (by buying Treasury securities). This helped Washington to spend more than it taxed American families and businesses. Such funding of the federal deficit was apparently "meddling" that did not trouble anyone. However, when interest rates on US Treasuries dropped and when the dollar (in which that interest was paid) declined, the UAE government decided not to keep so much wealth in US Treasuries. A growing portion was to be moved into the sovereign funds that buy stocks, bonds, and companies.

Countries whose sovereign funds exceed $100 billion today include the UAE, Singapore, Saudi Arabia, Norway, Kuwait, and Russia, while China will likely soon join this group. Many other countries have sovereign funds still below $100 billion. When such funds buy controlling interest in companies, it represents a kind of "nationalization of formerly private enterprises." In this way, governments may wield direct economic power and thereby the political influence that Lawrence Summers fears. Yet, governments in most advanced industrial economies have long been influencing foreign and domestic firms active in their countries. By doing so, governments also influence enterprises in other countries. The sovereign funds are just another way that governments will exert economic influence in other countries. The question is, so what?

Power and wealth are interactive and interdependent. America maintains a US Treasury Office charged with examining and approving foreign purchases of assets and firms. The Committee on Foreign Investment in the US (CFIUS) checks all purchases to assure they don't compromise national security or technological leadership. The US government exercises power over the value of the US dollar, which directly influences the wealth of individuals, companies, and governments around the world. All governments own parts of or entire companies inside their countries; only the extent of government ownership varies. The US, EU, Japanese, Australian, Korean governments are now directly influencing troubled banks with eased credit and will likely do more to ease a growing financial crisis. Governments have been "meaningful actors" in their own and others' economies for a long time. Sovereign funds are just another ownership structure in an old story.

At the same time, businesses wield political influence. They seek to lower their taxes, increase their subsidies, best competitors, open new markets, and so on, by lobbying, bribing, and otherwise "meddling" in politics. Business requires and rewards political meddling. And the goal of political meddling by business is to shape the economic meddling by the government. Such mutual meddling is governed by the mechanisms and pressures of national and international laws and markets. For a long time, it has made little difference whether the company was owned by private individuals or state officials, foreign or domestic.

For example, some years ago, the Renault automobile company purchased American Motors. In pursuing profitability for American Motors, Renault meddled in US politics in the same ways used by American Motors before Renault's purchase. Renault was then partly owned by the French government, but that made very little difference. The workers performed their tasks as they always had. The board of directors selected by the French government did nothing basically different from what the board of directors elected by American Motors shareholders had done.

Of course, some particular US industries and companies may be adversely affected by sovereign funds' investments in the US. That is, they will face more or strengthened competition of various kinds. They may then try to prevent sovereign funds from investing in the US or demand tight limits on their activities. Other US industries and companies will see advantages in sovereign funds' arrival. The corporations who expect to benefit from sovereign funds' activities in the US will fight against those who expect to suffer. Both sets of companies will meddle in US and foreign government activity to achieve their goals.

The two sides will fight for or against US laws regulating sovereign funds. To win, each side will have to meddle (i.e., mobilize political support). That means spending money to lobby legislators and to "shape public opinion." The companies favoring the sovereign funds' entry will flood the media with stories about the copious benefits that will flow. The companies opposed to sovereign funds will spread alarms about "foreign" meddling that "threatens our way of life." They will find allies among Americans who displace their real problems onto fears of "foreigners" and/or "foreign governments." Each side will buy its academic spokespersons to put a veneer of expertise on its public relations. Some may even try to place stories in the *New York Times* written by prominent experts to influence popular opinion.

We know the game plan because we have seen it all before. Years ago, opposing groups of companies squared off over NAFTA. The side with the most money to spend and the best public relations strategies won. Repeatedly over the decades, the struggle between the companies who want "free trade" and those who seek "protection" reworks the same game plan. Among the relatively few directly affected by such corporate struggles, some will gain and some will lose. For most Americans, the outcomes of these struggles make relatively little lasting difference. So it will be again in the looming struggle over sovereign funds. After all, they have been around quite a while. The UAE set up its sovereign fund in 1976; Singapore in 1974, Kuwait in 1960. They always aimed to make money within existing global capitalism, not to change it, and certainly not to threaten it. Those goals drive their activities inside the US as well.

The American people have real and pressing economic and political concerns; job and pay security, basic human services, and deepening inequality might start the list. These are far more urgent than choosing sides in a media-hyped corporate fight over sovereign funds.

US Economic Slide Threatens Mexico

1 September 2008

Deteriorating economic and social conditions in Mexico have generated mounting social problems. Private enterprises in Mexico and the government they control cannot manage, let alone solve them. Huge demonstrations are rocking the country with more to come. One chief cause of Mexico's problems is the turmoil and decline in the US economy. Rising US unemployment lessens its appeal for poor Mexicans seeking to escape their country's gross economic inequalities and lack of opportunity for a decent life. Cash that Mexican immigrants in the US send back to their families—"remittances" is its formal name—has stopped growing and begun a significant decline. What were major offsets to Mexico's disastrous economic conditions—sending able-bodied workers out of the country and then siphoning part of their US earnings back into it—have changed into their opposites: threats to destabilize Mexican society.

For many years, the US official policy toward Mexico was based on choosing between Mexican economic and social instability and allowing Mexican immigration into the US. Republicans and Democrats alike consistently chose immigration. It solved the economic problems of a Mexican capitalism that was and remains extremely unjust in its distributions of wealth, income, and well-being and extremely inefficient in utilizing its labor force. First, migration to the US gave desperate Mexicans, and especially men, a way to escape that country's failure to provide decent jobs or incomes to millions of its citizens. Mexico thus exported what might otherwise have become a politically dangerous mass critical of Mexican capitalism. Second, it generated those remittances back into Mexico that kept afloat an economy that would otherwise have provoked social unrest and revolutionary movements among those unable or unwilling to emigrate to the US. Both mass emigration and massive remittances kept the Mexican economic disaster from becoming an active social crisis on the US border.

Immigration likewise suited US businesses by providing millions of new workers (especially those immigrants fearful about their illegal status) willing to accept lower wages and benefits than were the US norm. All sorts of gains accrued to US employers of Mexican immigrants (in agriculture, construction, retail, and beyond). Vast profits were made by the US financial companies through whom Mexican immigrants sent their remittances home. A recent World Bank report found that banks and other agencies (such as Western Union) charged an average of 4 to 8 percent of each remittance as payment for transferring the money from the US to Mexico (a trivial and nearly costless electronic transfer process). Such employers made sure that anti-Mexican immigrant policies were never effective.

There were the usual hyped public relations gestures by politicians pandering to US movements against Latino immigration. However, business interests, the immigrant communities themselves, and liberal groups prevailed against those movements. The inflow of Mexican immigrants and the outflow of remittances to Mexico were not stopped by political means. It has been US capitalism's credit meltdown and its consequences that have changed the economic links between Mexico and the US.

The dependence of Mexico's extremely unequal capitalism on emigration and remittances is stark. In the most thorough study to date, the World Bank's Raul Hernandez-Coss found that in 2003, remittances were a much larger inflow of money into Mexico than both foreign tourist expenditures inside Mexico and total foreign direct investment in Mexico.

That has remained the case through 2007. Only oil exports brought in a bit more money than workers' remittances. And the prospects for Mexico's future oil production are declining while those for many other Mexican exports are being dimmed by devastating competition from Chinese and other Asian exports.

Remittances grew many times faster—peaking at $24 billion in 2006—than gross domestic product in Mexico over the last decade, thus becoming an ever more important support for an otherwise increasingly dysfunctional economy. The consensus estimate of researchers is that 20 percent of Mexican families—many among the nation's poorest—now depend significantly on remittances for their basic incomes. Since many transfers are made through illegal and other channels not counted by the gatherers of statistics, it is certain that all official estimates are in fact *under*estimates of the actual remittance flows and their importance.

On July 30, 2008, the Mexican central bank reported a 3-percent drop in remittances this year. As jobs shrink in the US economy—initially in the construction and housing industries and then spreading to the retail and other industries that employ many Mexican immigrants—immigration into the US is slowing and remittance flows to Mexico will shrink further. Either alone is a threat to Mexico; both together may explode its economy and society.

Already the signs of explosion are proliferating. Drug traffic and the vast network of employment opportunities it generates in Mexico are growing far faster than the Mexican government can manage. Crime is so widespread and the corruption it generates is so deeply entrenched among business leaders and government agencies that mass demonstrations demand increasingly basic change just when economic flows steadily worsen Mexico's social situation.

Globalized capitalism is a chain as strong as its weakest link. The economic crisis that began with the sub-prime mortgage collapse in the US has since spread via the globalized credit and trade system to the rest of the world. Its terrible economic and social costs and consequences will soon expose the currently weakest links in the chain. Mexico may prove to be one of them.

PART III: POLITICS OF THE CRISIS

Politically, workers and consumers, business, and governments reacted differently to the reality of today's capitalist crisis. Before the crisis hit, great majorities of all three groups believed (1) that no crisis would occur, (2) that if one occurred it would be short and shallow, and/or (3) that the government could and would easily contain any economic downturn. Such perspectives were informed by the mainstream economic theories discussed in essays in Part II. Part III, the politics of the crisis, discusses the different political reactions to the crisis as it evolved since the end of 2007.

The government reacted (Bush) and continues to react (Obama) by means of massive rescues of enterprises deemed "too big to fail," broad fiscal stimuli, and the imposition of new rules and regulations. Some essays in Part II addressed the rescues; in Part III essays directly address fundamental flaws in the political program of responding to capitalist crises with reforms and regulations. Those flaws refer to how business and government are now struggling and maneuvering to shape temporary versus long-term government interventions prompted by this crisis. The essays demonstrate the historical repetition of these struggles and draw certain conclusions relevant to politics today.

The unfolding capitalist crisis has produced a number of renewals and rediscoveries of non- or anti-capitalist solutions for capitalist crises. "Socialism" has re-entered public discussion in the wake of the crisis, partly because right-wing organizations and media attacked Obama as a socialist, and partly because so serious a crisis of capitalism directs attention to possible alternative economic systems. Several essays in Part III explore the different meanings and implications of socialist solutions. Several other essays explore the relevance of anti-capitalist theory and practice to workers and consumers impacted by capitalism as a system, especially when it is in crisis. These essays begin a return to the past "great debates" about capitalism, socialism, and communism on the grounds of their immediate pertinence.

1. Reforms and Regulations as Crisis Solutions

Economic Reforms: Been There, Done That

14 April 2008

Markets are key to the current economic meltdown. First, the US real estate market drove up prices and provoked fantasies that unprecedented prices would not collapse. Then markets reversed and plunged us into recession. The misnamed "sub-prime mortgage" crisis began by hobbling mortgage brokers and lenders and big investment banks. Their huge losses were then spread, by the world's integrated capital markets, to yield a general "credit crunch" crippling countless other lenders and borrowers. Now, the links among credit and output markets have brought recession, rising bankruptcy, and falling employment. US households, for the first time in history, now spend more of their disposable income to pay off debts (14 percent) than to buy food (13 percent).

In such conditions, the primary concern of corporate executives and politicians has been to blame others. Their favorite targets are the economic version of "a few bad apples," namely those "sub-prime" borrowers who took out mortgages they could not afford and those greedy lenders who "may have" connived with them.

After blame, the next priority is to "solve" the economic problems by means of "economic reforms." Calls for them are growing everywhere. Reform proposals list steps for corporations and/or the government to take to regulate and control credit markets "so that they will work better and not repeat the current mess." Those who resist market reforms and cling to the old mantra of "free markets" as "efficient" feel ever more isolated and marginalized.

Yet, economic reforms deserve a "been there, done that" dismissal. Past reforms, emerging from past economic crises, have repeatedly failed to prevent subsequent crises. For example, in recent years over 90 percent of all US mortgage borrowers were required to sign and deliver a special Internal Revenue Service document (IRS Form 4506T) to their lenders.

The form allowed lenders to access borrowers' tax filings to verify their incomes—and thus their ability to afford the mortgages. According to Gretchen Morgenson (*New York Times*, 6 April 2008), *most lenders never checked with the IRS because they deliberately ignored borrowers' limitations*. Because lenders profitably resold mortgages immediately after borrowers signed them, they cared little about risky borrowers. The corporations that bought those mortgages packaged them into securities they resold globally to banks and other investors. High ratings and insurance policies attached to those securities hid their riskiness. Profits were the carrot and competition was the stick driving each corporate player in the system.

Past reforms (such as IRS Form 4506T) failed, not because some shaky borrowers and a few shady lenders evaded them, but because our economic system drives all players to take and hide risks that markets then spread globally. The system generates crises, then ineffective reforms, and then crises again. It is a *systemic* failure when 90 percent of lending corporations ignore past reforms aimed to control their behavior and thereby prevent economic disaster. However, the system that failed is not primarily the market. The roots of dysfunction lie elsewhere in the corporate structure of capitalist enterprises.

Contemporary lenders are chiefly large corporations (banks, brokerages, mortgage lenders, etc.) whose boards of directors (usually comprising 15 to 20 individuals) appropriate an immense mass of profits. Competition presses them to seek ever more profits. So they lend unwisely, producing financial crises. Then reforms are passed to cope with these crises. Invariably, the affected corporations use their profits to minimize the reforms' effect on their profitable activities, or to evade the reforms, or to persuade politicians to "adjust" or repeal the reforms. Past "reforms" always failed because they left in place the old corporate structure with the same incentive (profits) and the same resources (profits) to undermine those reforms one way or the other. This then set the stage for the next crisis.

Given the inadequacy of past reforms, will yet another set of them be passed now? Or can we finally make the necessary systemic changes to both the corporate structure of business and the relationship between business and society? And what might they be?

The first systemic change would affect productive workers—those who actually make the goods and services that corporations then sell to get "their" profits. Such workers would become their own collective board of directors. Corporations would then no longer have tiny boards of directors (elected by and accountable to shareholders) that extract profits, control workers, and dominate politics and culture. By making productive workers and directors the same group of people, wages and working conditions would suddenly become as important as profits to decision makers.

The second systemic change would subject these new workers/directors to a social system of checks and balances governing their economic decisions. They would have to share the power to decide how much work will be done, how much profit will be made, and how the profits will be distributed and used across the society. The workers/directors would share such decision-making with several groups, other "stakeholders" who likewise depend on the results of such decisions.

These other groups include, firstly, all those workers who do not directly produce goods and services, but rather provide the conditions for—enable—production to occur. Such enablers include, for example, the clerks, sales, and purchasing personnel, wholesale and retail merchants, secretaries, bank workers, and so on. Other enablers are workers in government and social welfare enterprises (public schools, hospitals, military, etc.). Beside such workers, local, state, and national communities would also join in democratically co-determining job conditions, the sizes of profits, and their disposition.

Finally, just as community members would share decision-making power inside enterprises with the workers, the latter would share decision-making powers over community affairs.

Such a worker-community system of checks and balances would democratize society's basic economic decisions—for the first time in history—as well as link them intimately with similarly organized social decisions.

With such a system of checks and balances, "transparency," and thus "accountability" might genuinely characterize economic decisions rather than being empty slogans covering corporate misdeeds. If, instead of making such systemic change, we lapse into another "reformism" during this present global economic downturn, we invite yet another systemic failure.

Regulations Do Not Prevent Capitalist Crises

14 April 2009

A huge chorus now clamors to heap new regulations on banks, credit markets, international capital flows, and so on. Regulations, for many in politics, the media, and academia, seem to have become the magic bullet that will not only "solve" the current economic crisis but also prevent future meltdowns. Many labor union and left voices agree.

FDR advocated his New Deal regulations in the same terms during the 1930s. Yet FDR's regulations failed to get the US out of the Great Depression and they obviously failed to prevent subsequent economic crises. Today's is the second major crash in 75 years, while nearly a dozen other, less severe downturns also occurred since the Great Depression. Regulations have repeatedly proved incapable of ending capitalism's inherent instability, its proclivity to boom and bust cycles with huge social costs.

Economic regulations fail because of two fatal flaws. First, they may be poorly enforced or simply ignored. When political conditions permit leaders to be selected and/or controlled by the enemies of regulation, they can block the state's enforcement of regulations. Second, even when politicians try to enforce regulations on corporations, they successfully evade, weaken, or eliminate most of them. It is the organization of capitalist enterprises that explains both flaws and their repeated sabotage of regulations.

Counter-recessionary regulations always more or less constrain corporations' freedom of action in pursuing market share and profits. However, past regulations stopped short of changing the basic structure of capitalist corporations (and so do those proposed by Obama). Thus, the vast majority of people participating in corporate enterprises, the workers, always exercised little or no control over the decisions governing what the enterprises would produce, how and where they would produce, and what would be done with the resulting profits.

Those decisions were always made by each corporation's board of directors, usually 15 to 20 individuals chosen by and responsible to the corporation's *major* shareholders. Shareholding in the US is highly concentrated. Federal Reserve data show that the vast majority of US families own either no shares or so small a portion of outstanding shares that they exercise little or no influence over the selection or the decisions of boards of directors.

Inside capitalist enterprises, the huge majority—the workers—depends on the jobs, incomes, and working conditions determined by the tiny minority, the board of directors. While the tenth of US workers who are unionized wield some limited influence over boards of directors, most US workers cannot participate in deciding the what, how, and where of production or how enterprise profits are used. The capitalist organization of enterprises is undemocratic. This lack of internal democracy dooms counter-recessionary regulations to failure.

From FDR to Obama, capitalist crashes brought state interventions into the economy that always included new or increased regulations. Immediately after (and sometimes already during) every phase of regulation, boards of directors and major shareholders of many US corporations began to undermine that regulation. They used corporate profits to pay for lobbying, publicity and mass media campaigns, think tank "research," and so on. By shaping public opinion and academic understanding, they persuaded politicians to ignore or minimally enforce the regulations. At the same time, they hired lawyers, accountants, and economists to evade the regulations and public relations experts to mask or justify their evasion. When politically feasible, their opposition to regulation ramped up another notch. They got Congress, federal agencies, and state and local governments to first weaken and eventually eliminate many regulations.

Corporate boards of directors have every incentive to undermine regulations that limit their profits and market share. Major shareholders demand that and reward them accordingly. Boards of directors have the corporate profits needed to finance the defeat of unwanted regulations. The capitalist structure of enterprises thus provided both the incentive and the means for corporations' boards of directors to undermine FDR's New Deal regulations. FDR's tragic legacy was preservation of the capitalist organization of enterprise, leaving in place the corporate boards of directors and major shareholders. If we say "shame on them" for undermining regulations imposed after capitalism's 1930s crash, we will have to say "shame on us" if we allow the same process to unfold now under Obama.

We cannot solve this systemic failure of regulations to stop capitalist crashes by more or different or stricter regulation. Corporations have demonstrated their drive and capacity to frustrate the regulation strategy. Nor is the solution a state take-over of enterprise. The histories of the USSR and China show that when state officials replace private corporation's boards of directors, what remains in place are antagonistic and undemocratic structures pitting workers against the small groups that make the key production decisions and distribute enterprise profits. State officials, like their private counterparts, frustrate and undermine regulations.

A different solution not yet tried offers us the best chance for success. It entails a radical reorganization of enterprises, whether owned and operated privately or by the state. Democratize the workplace by replacing boards of directors or state officials with the workers themselves functioning collectively as their own board of directors.

Enterprises reorganized in this way would have objectives and reward systems, incentives and means to realize them that would all differ from those of capitalist enterprises where workers confront others who make the key economic decisions. Workers who were also their own board of directors would be less likely to disregard the effects (economic, environmental, cultural, and political) of workplace decisions on surrounding communities (where the workers and their families themselves live). Such workers would aim more for securer jobs and rising wages than for rising profits or market shares.

Such a democratization of the workplace would dovetail much more smoothly with genuinely democratic politics: workers accustomed to democracy on the job would more likely resist its exclusion from their residential communities. Economic democracy and political democracy are conditions of each other's existence. The interdependence of workplace conditions and community conditions would require and thus likely promote continuous negotiation between their separate yet overlapping democratic organizations. The regulations that emerged from such negotiations would more likely be respected and enforced by workers-qua-directors than the regulations that were negated so regularly by non-worker boards across the last century.

Why not move beyond the capitalist form of enterprises, whether private or state? We have nothing to lose but our capitalist crises. We have a new world economy to win.

2. Debates over "Socialist" Solutions

Economic Crisis, Ideological Debates

23 September 2008

In US capitalism's greatest financial crisis since the 1930s Depression, status-quo ideology swirls. The goal is to keep this crisis under control, to prevent it from challenging capitalism itself. One method is to keep public debate from raising the issue of whether and how class changes—basic economic system changes—might be the best "solution." Right, center, and even most left commentators exert that ideological control, some consciously and some not.

Hence the debates pitting those demanding more or better government regulation against those who insist that unregulated private enterprises operating in free markets work best. Both sides limit the public discussion about saving the economy to more vs. less state intervention. Then, too, we have quarrels over details of state intervention: the politicians promise help for foreclosure victims, limits on financiers' pay packages, and the thorough weeding out of bad apples, while spokespersons of various financial enterprises struggle to shape the details to their particular interests.

We need to recall that crises always generate "solutions"— like all those above—that preserve the basic system. We also need to advance alternatives not subordinated to the status quo, that open up the discussion by showing the risks of *not* changing the system and the virtues of doing so.

Let's begin with the issue of government regulation. Note first that corporations like investment banks, commercial banks, stock and mortgage brokerages, and so on are all run by boards of directors. These boards make our economic system's key decisions: they hire the millions who do the work, decide on the disposition of profits, and so on. Today's financial mess and economic crisis are first and foremost results of decisions by these boards of directors.

In previous economic crises—especially the 1930s Depression—financial corporations were subjected to government laws and regulations passed under pressure of mass suffering. However, the politicians who wrote those laws and regulations soon thereafter allowed financial corporations to evade them, then later to amend them, and finally to eliminate many of them. Politicians accommodated financial corporations because they were major contributors to their campaigns and major supports of their political careers or because they believed government intervention to always be "bad" for economic well-being. Financial corporations' directors used profits also to hire armies of lobbyists who shaped every government step in deciding whether and how to enforce laws, rewrite regulations, etc. Thus, US regulators depended increasingly on the financial corporations they supposedly regulated. Nor should we forget the profits financial corporations have always devoted to "public relations"—costly campaigns to undermine the very idea of government regulation in school curricula, mass media, politics, and across our culture. So now we return to square one as deregulated finance—having done its job of making billions for the industry—produces another crisis and another set of calls for regulation.

In short, arguing over whether to leave finance to financial corporations or to have government regulate them is no real debate. In the US, financial corporations' boards of directors have dominated the operations of the financial industries either way. Since all regulations imposed on US financial enterprises have left their boards of directors as sole receivers and distributors of all profits, the boards used them to evade or gut the regulations. What the right, center, and left now debate is merely another set of regulations, all of which again leave untouched the profits accruing to financial companies' boards of directors.

Finance has been grossly mismanaged by the institution of the corporation under deregulation: hence the crisis. Responding to this fact requires more than government reregulation. We need also to change the corporation in basic ways that can avoid or correct financial mismanagement. Nothing could better assure that new and tougher government regulations might work this time than *making the workers inside financial corporations real partners with the government in monitoring and enforcing properly regulated financial activities*.

To that end, a radical restructuring of financial corporations could require that their employees at all levels become major participants in decision-making activity. That means elevating workers to significant membership on boards of directors and all board committees. Only then can employees know corporate realities and so make sure financial activities conform to the spirit and letter of regulations. Only then will inappropriate activities get reported to and investigated by regulators long before they accumulate into today's sort of crisis. Masses of employees institutionally empowered inside corporate decision-making are the nation's best hope for a better, fairer financial system than we have had to date.

In short, if the US government—ultimately the taxpayers—will now pay the costs and take the risks to bail out a failed financial system, then it has the right and obligation to change that system. We need such changes to avoid repeating the failures of the past. These changes would also introduce some democracy inside the corporation—where it has been excluded for too long and with disastrous consequences.

The current debates also fail to face how the underlying economy helped produce the financial mess. Real wages stopped rising in the US in the 1970s, yet the American psyche and self-image, subject to relentless advertising, was committed to rising consumption. To enable that, workers with flat wages had to borrow to afford rising consumption. For the last 30 years loans replaced wages, but rising consumer debt introduces new risks and dangers. If, simultaneously, politicians use state borrowing to avoid taxing the rich while providing vast corporate subsidies and waging endless wars, the debt problems mushroom. Aggressive, deregulated financial companies grabbed the resulting "market opportunity" by devising ever more complex, hidden, and dangerously risky ways to profit hugely from the social debt bubble.

A sub-prime economy produced sub-prime wages, sub-prime borrowers, sub-prime lenders, and sub-prime government regulation. Bailing out and reregulating financiers—the current plan being debated across the nation—does far too little too late. The proposal above exemplifies the much bigger and more basic changes that now need active public discussion.

Socialism's New American Opportunity

27 November 2008

The US left today confronts a remarkable opportunity. George Bush and Sarah Palin effectively reopened the explicit debate over capitalism versus socialism. More than that, their interventions, combined with the current crisis of capitalism, disrupt the conventional, classic definitions of both isms. Thus, the debate over them is now transformed in advantageous ways for the US left.

Sarah Palin tried to attach the epithet "socialist" to Obama during the campaign. She linked it to his remark about a modest tax reform that might "spread the wealth" a bit. McCain likewise jumped on the remark in ways that echoed Palin's effort. Clearly the Republicans' campaign saw an opportunity to damage Obama's candidacy. In a society that had, since 1989, successfully pushed the concepts of socialism and communism off the radar as historically "failed experiments," suddenly the mass media widely repeated affirmations that socialism was back again. For those who denounce as socialism any government program benefitting the middle and poor at the expense of the rich, the socialist threat seemed alive and well in the Obama camp. For Obama's supporters, they suddenly had to interrogate, even if only briefly and superficially, their own sense of and attitude toward the capitalism versus socialism debate.

Another reinsertion of the capitalism-versus-socialism debate into contemporary American society followed from the Bush administration's response to the economic crisis. Bush made a November 13, 2008, speech that included these lines: "But the crisis was not a failure of the free market system. And the answer is not to try to reinvent that system." That day's Associated Press coverage (by Ben Feller) made sure to identify what "system" Bush meant; Feller's story was entitled: "Bush defends capitalism on eve of economic summit." The president most Americans had just repudiated at the polls was defending capitalism. Might anti-Bush voters, consciously or otherwise, consider also rejecting what he was defending?

Bush raised the capitalism versus socialism issue in yet another way. Over the last few months his administration has violated in its practice the neoliberal dogma about the absolute superiority of private enterprise and markets. While that dogma still gets Bush's lip service, his "economic team" has forcibly converted private into state-run enterprises (including the largest US insurance company, AIG, the largest mortgage lenders, Fannie Mae and Freddy Mac, and the largest US banks, Citibank, Bank of America, and so on). Republican fiscal conservatives are running up humongous deficits borrowing trillions to finance state-planned "bailouts" that hand vast sums to selected firms. Government planning is replacing markets in determining an increasing number of transactions and thus the course of the national economy.

Displacing private in favor of state property and markets in favor of state planning are the sins usually charged to socialism by the conservative supporters of capitalism. How then are people to make sense of the Bush government's embrace of just those sins? Does a capitalist crisis require a dose of socialism as its solution? And what might that suggest?

Across the country, many people's thoughts and conversations, as widely reported in the media, have raised questions about capitalism and socialism in their relation to the Bush past and the Obama future. Yet this turn is happening because of events that throw the conventional definitions of socialism into considerable doubt and disarray. Leftists particularly are uncomfortable with describing Obama as a socialist, and not only because of the context and purpose of Palin's charge. They are also uneasy about how to assess the Bush regime's massive turn toward state ownership and planning at the expense of private ownership and free markets.

The return of "socialism" to the thinking and conversations of many Americans is an exceptional opportunity for the left. Beyond scoffing at Palin's charge and Bush's economics, leftists now have an exceptional opportunity to explain how "socialism" can and should mean something more than and different from progressive tax reforms, state ownership of enterprises, and state planning of economic affairs. However, the need to produce a definition of socialism as "something more" confronts some traditional definitions that do focus on progressive state economic policy interventions (such as tax reform) and/or state ownership and planning.

To make the most of this historical period's opportunity would require the left to formulate a new concept of and vision for socialism. For example, if socialism were defined to include the following basic reorganization inside enterprises, no one would confuse it with anything done by Bush or advocated by Obama. Suppose socialism were defined in the following terms: (1) the workers in every enterprise must function collectively as their own board of directors and as the private owners of their enterprise; (2) democratically elected local, regional, and national political bodies would share with each enterprise's workers the power to determine production methods and the disposition of outputs and revenues; and (3) democratically elected representatives of the workers in each enterprise would share with residentially elected political bodies the power to determine political issues. Defined in this way, socialism would entail a specific kind of interconnected democratization of the economy and the society. The residential community and the workforce, as stakeholders, would share the power of deciding basic social issues.

This is, of course, only one among many examples of rethinking socialism. The point is to extend and refocus the current public considerations of whether and how the term could and should apply to the US. The left might thereby take advantage of an ironic reopening of these considerations by socialism's enemies. Indeed, such a rethinking now in the US could also finally settle accounts with what actually happened in and to the "socialisms" of the USSR and China. And the point of it all would be to refashion socialism to contest effectively for hearts and minds now opened by capitalism's worst crisis in decades.

Those Alternative Socialist "Stimulus" Plans

22 February 2009

There are, of course, *other* ways to "support and stimulate" the declining US economy: those that congressional debaters, presidential advisors, and the dutiful media never discuss. All the Federal Reserve and the US Treasury ever do is justify their functions as lenders and spenders "of last resort" (when the private sector will not). Neither ever mentions that the state could stimulate the economy if it became the employer and producer of last resort (when the private sector lays off and cuts back). The carefully stage-managed passage of Obama's economic policy package avoided any troubling consideration of all the stimulus roads *not* taken.

The various sorts of more-or-less socialist alternatives are reviving from 30 years of hibernation. They swirl just below the surface of public life: direct products of global capitalism's deepening crisis and the continuing failure of official US policy responses. Soon those alternatives will enter the public consciousness and debate here as they already did in Latin America, Europe, and elsewhere. The anti-capitalist demonstrations, general strikes, and new political movements abroad that raise socialist demands there have their impacts here too.

One kind of socialism—that focused on nationalizing formerly private enterprises—has already broken through in the US. The government nationalized some large financial enterprises and public debates weigh more nationalization in finance, in the auto industry, and beyond. The knee-jerk accusation—that such talk is socialistic—no longer stops the debates. Where, we may wonder, will nationalization stop?

Another kind of socialism remains taboo—state hiring of workers for whom no private sector jobs exist. That idea is still unspeakable. The fact that FDR did it in the depths of the Great Depression makes no difference *yet*. Hiring the unemployed for state jobs would put the money paid for their wages directly into circulation (which is what loans to banks failed to do). It would immediately mean many resumed mortgage payments and many fewer foreclosures.

Growing state employment may confront private capitalist corporations with new competition. Fear of that competition trumps those corporations' desires for the new customers that a state jobs program would provide. So most media keep mum about a mass government jobs program and officials follow suit. However, just as what was unspeakable six months ago—bank nationalization—is being discussed now, the ban on discussing public employment for the privately unemployed may be broken soon.

Then there are socialists for whom nationalization and public employment programs are not enough. Their preferred stimulus program would go beyond lending and spending more and taxing less (policies so far unsuccessful). They want to *reorganize production*—to change how goods and services get produced—as well as employ more people. The change they favor would establish state enterprises where workers function as their own collective board of directors—rather than having directors be other people accountable to shareholders and/or government officials. They would likewise provide financial incentives for parallel reorganizations in private enterprises. For them, replacing a capitalist organization of production by a socialist one is the best solution for today and for a future freed from capitalism's crisis-prone instability.

For example, socialists who focus on reorganizing production point out that had workers been their own directors in the 1970s, they would not have stopped raising workers' real wages while their productivity kept rising. If wages had not stagnated since the 1970s, neither household debt nor corporate profits would have soared to dangerous, unsustainable levels. They link those profits to the stock market bubble that burst in 2000, and they link out-of-control debt plus wild financial industry profits to the real estate bubble that burst in 2007–2008. These socialists also argue that enterprises run by their employees would be less likely than capitalist firms to fire workers, foreclose on homes, and move production overseas: actions that today spread and deepen the economic crisis. Lastly, the production reorganization these socialists propose would require workers to become skilled at boards of directors' tasks (deciding what to produce, where, and how; and distributing the profits). They cap their argument by saying that economic democracy on the job is a condition for real (as opposed to merely formal) democracy in politics.

Remarkably, one part of Obama's just-passed stimulus program does *combine* an immediate crisis response (establishing a new health program that will inject more money into the economy) with reorganizing part of the economy. A new federal research council will get $1.1 billion to "compare drugs, medical devices, surgery, and other ways of treating specific conditions." Beyond stimulating the economy by hiring researchers, buying equipment, etc., the new council also begins to reorganize healthcare by evaluating and publicly reporting which among competing treatments for a disease is actually the most effective. If allowed to function, this new council will challenge many corporate advertising claims for the medicines, medical devices, etc. that they sell. Independently determining and publicizing the best treatments could lower huge US medical costs for individuals and businesses (which far exceed those in all other advanced industrial economies). Of course, corporations that fear losing sales will likely undermine the new council.

Corporations will also fight efforts by socialists to reorganize production. Capitalist enterprises would be threatened because inside reorganized enterprises—let's call them socialist—worker/directors would create very different working conditions for worker/employees. Because workers in socialist enterprises would be treated differently, they would produce different qualities of output and use the profits of their enterprises in different ways. Suppose capitalist enterprises had to compete on a level playing field with such socialist enterprises. US consumers would then have real choices—for the first time—between goods and services depending on what kind of production organization they emerge from (much as they can now choose depending on where commodities are produced, how organically they are produced, whether they are fair-traded, etc.). US workers would then have real choices—for the first time— between alternative work lives.

In response to today's capitalist crisis, government policy could move in socialist directions toward more nationalization, more public employment, and a socialist reorganization of production. This policy would combine an immediate crisis response with solutions for its longer-run causes and deeper foundations. By avoiding and delaying the public debate over such socialist policy alternatives, the powers that be subject the vast majority to the ever larger social costs of their system's crisis.

Wanted: Red-Green Alliance for Radically Democratic Reorganization of Production

29 March 2009

Private capitalism (in which productive assets are owned by private individuals and groups and in which markets rather than state planning dominate the distribution of resources and products) has repeatedly demonstrated a tendency to flare out into overproduction and/or asset inflation bubbles that burst with horrific social consequences. Endless reforms, restructurings, and regulations were all justified in the name not only of extricating us from a crisis but also finally preventing future crises (as Obama repeated this week). They all failed to do that.

The tendency to crisis seems unstoppable, an inherent quality of capitalism. At best, the beginnings of crises were caught before they wreaked major havoc, although usually that only postponed and aggravated that havoc. One recent case in point: the stock market crash of early 2000 was limited in its damaging social consequences (recession, etc.) by an historically unprecedented reduction of interest rates and money supply expansion by Alan Greenspan's Federal Reserve. The resulting real estate bubble temporarily offset the effects of the stock market's bubble bursting, but when real estate crashed a few years later, what had been deferred hit catastrophically.

Repeated failure to stop its inherent crisis tendency is beginning to tell on the system. The question increasingly insinuates itself even into discourses with a long history of denying its pertinence: has capitalism, qua system, outlived its usefulness?

Repeated state interventions to rescue private capitalism from its self-destructive crises or from the political movements of its victims yielded longer or shorter periods of state capitalism (in which productive assets are owned or significantly controlled or regulated by state officials and in which state planning dominates markets as mechanisms of resource and product distribution). Yet state capitalisms have not solved the system's crisis tendencies either. That is why they have repeatedly given way to oscillations back to private capitalism (e.g. the Reagan "revolution" in the US, the end of the USSR, etc.).

Moreover, the history of FDR's efforts to counteract the Great Depression teaches fundamental lessons about capitalism as a system. Since the New Deal reforms all stopped short of transforming the structure of corporations, they left in place the corporate boards of directors and shareholders who had both the incentives and resources to evade, undermine, and abolish those reforms. Evasion was their focus until the 1970s, and abolition since. Capitalism systematically organizes its key institutions of production—the corporations—in such a way that their boards of directors, *in properly performing their assigned tasks*, produce crises, then undermine anti-crisis reforms, and thereby reproduce those crises.

Hence, attention is slowly shifting to questioning the one aspect of capitalism that was never effectively challenged, let alone changed, across the last century and more: the internal organization of corporations. Their decisions about what, where, and how to produce and how to utilize profits are all made not by the mass of workers, nor by the communities they impact, but rather by a board of directors. Composed typically of 15–20 individuals, corporate boards are tiny elites responsible to only the slightly larger elites comprising corporations' major shareholders. Each corporate board is charged by its major shareholders with maximizing profit, market share, growth, or share price. The mass of workers has to live with the results of board decisions over which they exercise next to no control. This is a position they share with the communities surrounding and dependent on those same corporations.

This capitalist organization of the corporation consistently generates investment, production, financial, marketing, and employment decisions that produce systemic instability—economic crises. This system's profoundly undemocratic organization of production demands radical transformation.

Suppose, as one such transformation, that workers undertook to function as their own board of directors. All weekly job descriptions would henceforth specify four days of particular production tasks and one day participating in collective decisions about what, how, and where to produce and what to do with profits. That means workers replacing the economic autocracy that structures capitalist corporations by democratic mechanisms, just as they have forced political autocracy to give way to democratic mechanisms. The economy and society would then evolve very differently from the capitalist pattern.

As every thinking person knows, climate change is upon us. Market solutions to stem it, which defenders of capitalism have proposed and implemented, have miserably failed to contain it. Substituting undemocratic state planning for markets is no solution either: one look at the environmental records of state planning in the former Eastern bloc suffices to corroborate this point. If we are to redesign our interactions with nature by taking account of the economic and environmental costs of energy sources, especially fossil fuels, as an increasing number of people recognize we must, why not redesign our enterprise structures to take account of the history of failed efforts to contain capitalism's crisis-producing dysfunction?

Might we consider a mutually beneficial alliance between critics of abusing our energy resources and critics of abusing our productive capabilities? How about an alliance focused on a radical, democratic, and therefore anti-capitalist reorganization of production? The point would be to make citizens and workers—those who must live with the results of what enterprises do—conjoint decision-makers focused on meeting collective needs, both productive and environmental.

Capitalist Crisis, Socialist Renewal

24 May 2009

This much is clear: not in a long time has capitalism been so critically questioned in the US and "socialism" so widely debated as a social alternative. The left can and should seize this moment. One part of doing that is to formulate a new program—including a new definition of socialism—that could grasp a mass consciousness, become central to public political debate, and inspire a new left mobilization in the US.

First, we need to settle our accounts with the (definitions and practices of) socialisms of the past. As Engels did in his *Socialism: Utopian and Scientific*, we need to state both what past socialisms accomplished and why they could not overcome and replace capitalism. Despite ruthless and implacable opposition, powerful labor, left, and socialist organizations were built and progressive social changes achieved. A rich left tradition of socialist criticism and analysis was created and spread globally. Across the nineteenth and twentieth centuries, the first wave of modern, anti-capitalist socialism became a global social force. However, where and when socialists made revolutionary breakthroughs against capitalism—whether or not they took state power—socialism's advances proved limited, vulnerable and therefore often temporary. The histories of the USSR and China, like those of socialist and communist programs and parties across the rest of the world, attest to distortions and reversals that enabled renewals of capitalism.

There were, of course, many contributors to socialism's history: those that impinged from outside and those that worked their effects from within. I am concerned here with the latter. Following Engel's model, I explore what has to change inside socialism to improve its chances to achieve new, further, and more secure breakthroughs in moving the human community beyond the injustice, limits, and costs of capitalism. Let's begin by subtitling the remainder of this short essay: *Socialism: Macro and Micro*.

Socialisms of the past focused on two broad social conditions: (1) the ownership of productive property, and (2) the mechanism of distributing productive resources and productive outputs. Capitalism was thus defined in terms of its reliance upon private ownership of productive property and markets. By contrast, socialism embraced socialized productive property and national economic planning (usually to be operated by a state apparatus controlled by socialists). Capitalism and socialism were thus differentiated in *macro* terms. What then did socialism mean at the *micro* level of society inside its individual enterprises?

The blunt answer is: not much. No clear differentiation of capitalism from socialism has so far emerged for the *internal* structures of enterprises. While socialists supported and often led workers' struggles for better wages and working conditions inside capitalist enterprises, their chief concerns were more macro-oriented. They sought to coordinate workers' struggles inside enterprises with developing political movements aimed to transform private into socialized property and markets into planning. Thus, when and where socialists became politically dominant, the basic internal structures of enterprises were not fundamentally altered. Laborers still finished their work days and departed, leaving behind their labors' fruits and leaving to others—boards of directors—the decisions about what to produce, how, and where, and what to do with the surpluses/profits. True, socialists emphasized state regulation of those boards' decisions or sometimes replaced private corporate boards of directors with state officials. However, the basic structures connecting workers to enterprise decision-makers remained, where socialists shaped them, markedly like their counterparts under capitalism.

In *Socialism: Utopian and Scientific*, Engels' key point was that many early socialists believed that powerful utopian visions of a better, post-capitalist society could not only capture people's imaginations but also thereby realize socialism. But utopian socialism, Engels argued, had not succeeded. Socialists therefore had to supplement it with a materialistically grounded (i.e. "scientific") strategy for practically transforming capitalism into socialism. Scientific socialism would identify key potential revolutionary agents and mobilize them politically for that transformation.

However, the macro focus of scientific socialism also proved inadequate to secure a transition from capitalism to socialism. It lacked the supplement of a micro focus, namely a definition of socialism at the level of each enterprise: specifically, that enterprises be reorganized such that the laborers become collectively their own board of directors. This micro dimension of socialism ends the classic divided organization of capitalist enterprises pitting those (the board of directors) who make the enterprise's key decisions against those who labor but do not make those decisions.

The full range of new strengths and potentials available to 21st-century socialism if it adds this micro dimension cannot be listed here, let alone elaborated. Consider just two examples. First, a macro-cum-micro socialism *institutionalizes* real worker participation in *all* aspects of production. Socialism will thereby mean that the workers themselves will be charged to transform the inherited capitalist enterprises by ending their divisions between manual and mental labor, directors and directed. Building a new socialist society will mean the workers' continuous role in reorganizing enterprises based on equality, sharing, or rotating all specific functions, and continuous collective decision-making. Socialism would then engage all workers in a life-long process of self-transformation alongside and intertwined with macro-level socialist transformation. The end result would equip and motivate workers to participate fully in politics and culture as well as in the economy.

Second, such a macro-cum-micro socialism can bring a concrete, practical meaning to otherwise often vague references to socialist "democracy." That kind of democracy would refer to how the collective of workers inside each enterprise reach all its key decisions. These enterprise collectives would necessarily enter into continuous deliberations and negotiations with one another and with similarly democratic collectives based on residency to reach genuinely democratic social decisions.

Utopian socialism contributed to the socialist tradition's growth and maturity, but its limits provoked a self-critique formulated around the concept of scientific socialism advocated by Marx and Engels. Scientific socialism then enhanced the tradition's further globalization and deepened both its theorizations and its practices. Nonetheless, scientific socialism has now outgrown its overly macro bias and thereby provoked another self-criticism. The result is the resolve to add the micro level so that the macro and micro levels will together provide at once the indispensable supports for, and also the democratic constraints on one another. Can such a reconstituted socialist conception and program also fail? Of course, but that is no argument against taking socialism another important step further just as the earlier socialists did. Today's global crisis exposes all of capitalism's fault lines, but it also offers socialists the chance to renew their project if they can learn and apply the lessons of socialism's history.

3. Anti-Capitalist Politics

Europe: Capitalism and Socialism

31 August 2005

In the spring of 2005, workers' votes in France and the Netherlands made the difference in defeating the draft European constitution and ending socialist party control of the German state of Baden-Wurttemberg. In the few weeks after those momentous events, most politicians and reporters offered one basic explanation. It tells us much more about the agenda of the explainers than about what is to be explained.

Their simple story proceeds in steps. First, European workers voted their anger over sustained high unemployment (read: workers see no farther than their paychecks). Second, that unemployment is the fault of Europe's social welfare programs and protection of workers' jobs and incomes. Third and final step: European workers must learn the "lessons of economic science" and thus recognize that "flexible labor markets" (read: sustained reductions in social welfare and worker protections) are the only way forward for European unity and prosperity.

This story crudely applies the neoliberal logic drawn from the standard elementary economics textbooks that now suffocate most university classrooms. It also misses the remarkable protest and change now unfolding in Europe, partly because it so uncritically embraces a deeply flawed neoliberal catechism.

The point of "flexible labor markets" is to enable employers to pay workers less, control them more, fire them more easily, and outsource where and when they choose: in short, employers want to replicate in continental Europe the conditions already enjoyed by their British and US competitors. Right away this would benefit employers and cost workers in Europe. It *might* in the long run also lead employers to hire more workers (since they can pay each worker less). It *might* in the long run increase the competitiveness and sales of European products (if employers lowered their prices or improved product quality). That is the rosy prediction and "analysis" offered by supporters of a neoliberal unified Europe. On the other hand, "flexible labor markets" *might* instead simply redistribute income, wealth, and power from workers to employers. It *might* drive workers to respond to lower and less secure wages by taking more jobs, laboring more hours, and borrowing massively to maintain their living standards. That, after all, has been the actual story of the US and UK over the last quarter century.

The logical flaw in neoliberalism is this: no one can know in advance all the economic and social effects of a "flexible labor market." No one can guarantee that what might happen actually will. To claim otherwise is not economic "science" but rather bought-and-paid-for economic propaganda. The key historically demonstrated facts are these: (1) employers pursue neoliberal "reform" to make more money and enhance their power, and (2) employers cannot control all the other effects of neoliberalism. The employers' political, journalistic, and academic supporters do not admit, let alone examine or document, the negative consequences that neoliberalism can deliver to workers.

That is why those supporters were surprised and challenged by the workers' votes in the recent European elections. Those workers' incomes and/or job securities had been reduced over recent years by neoliberal "reforms" identified as necessary for European "unity." So they worked more and took on debt. Their mounting stress strained family life and reduced civic participation. Such painful adjustments, as always, bred social tensions. Nationalist and right-wing leaders found opportunities to deflect workers' mounting anger about deteriorating economic and social conditions against immigrant communities and job outsourcing. However, workers with no affection for the right also found the dominant neoliberal conception of European unity increasingly unacceptable.

In this situation, the left in European politics began an historic split that became very public in the recent French, German, and Dutch elections. Especially inside the large socialist parties, those workers who opposed the neoliberal unification of Europe turned against the leaders who supported it by voting "no" on the proposed new (and neoliberal) European constitution. Because Germany's socialist leader, Gerhard Schroeder, did not allow a plebiscite on the new constitution, workers opposed to it expressed themselves by voting the socialist party down in Baden-Wurttemberg. The party immediately split with the departure of their popular leader Oskar Lafontaine who declared his interest in working with the further left Party of Democratic Socialism (now the Left Party) for a different kind of unified Europe. In France, millions of socialists voted against the new constitution, thereby directly contradicting their party leaders' support for it. This immediately opened the political space for a new left political effort combining disaffected socialists with the French Communist Party, which opposed the new constitution.

It remains to be seen whether and how the new political situation and possibilities will be realized. An emergent new left would need to design a systematic alternative to neoliberal European unification and communicate it effectively to the voters. To do this, it will have no option but to return to the basic class issues that capitalist development itself has returned to the forefront of European politics.

Europe's capitalists want neoliberal unification to enable them to compete effectively with non-European capitalists. As the latter do in their countries, European capitalists want freely to confront European workers with a simple threat: either accept less or we move production abroad. European capitalists promote a unification whose implications for European workers could not be clearer or starker. If European workers and their organizations capitulate, they will accelerate the downward spirals of wage loss, job insecurities, deepening debts, and social stresses that are already the capitalist norm elsewhere.

The only other option for a new European left is to rediscover the socialist alternative and adjust it to the new conditions. This will require confronting capitalists with a counter-threat: either maintain our hard-won working conditions, job protections, and social benefits or else we remove capitalists from their ownership and control of European productive enterprises. Since European capitalists will likely reject the threat, European socialists will need to draw and implement the hard lessons from the successes and failures of the last century's socialist experiments. They will need to mobilize working-class solidarity without obliterating differences, debates, and the space for initiatives from below. They will need to develop modes of organizing productive enterprises that will make the workers their own bosses. The issues of socializing productive property, democratically planning the economy, and above all, ending class exploitation will once again rise to the highest priority of political debate and struggle.

The remarkable historical twist here should not be missed. It was the rise of capitalism in Europe that produced socialism as its self-criticism, the profoundest contradiction and alternative to capitalism. In the intervening decades, capitalism and socialism became global. The rest of the world played its unique and powerful roles in shaping both global capitalism and global socialism. By the end of the twentieth century, global socialism encountered extreme problems and suffered many reverses. Global capitalism rejoiced at its sudden chance to expand again and seemingly without criticism or opposition. It proclaimed itself as the end of history, socialism as forever defeated, and the neoliberal phase of global capitalism as the unstoppable wave of the future. How remarkable that it is once again in Europe—although not now, of course, in Europe alone—that a new movement of socialist criticism is emerging. Produced by the latest neoliberal phase of capitalism, it may well become its greatest challenger yet, and this time perhaps its gravedigger.

The Urban Renewal Scam for New Orleans

17 September 2005

The old "urban renewal" scam is being born again in New Orleans. A hurricane, a flood, and a botched government response have combined to make the miracle possible. One of New Orleans' wealthy elite told Christopher Cooper of the *Wall Street Journal* ("Old-Line Families Escape Worst of Flood and Plot the Future," 8 September 2005): "New Orleans is ready to be rebuilt." Another elite member told Cooper that New Orleans had to be rebuilt more to his liking—"demographically, geographically and politically"—or folks like him would leave. As a wealthy New Orleans lawyer who raises funds for the Democratic Party told the same reporter, the mass evacuation of the poor could change New Orleans from a Democratic to a Republican stronghold.

New Orleans is now replaying perfectly the history of "urban renewal" in the US. No doubt, New Orleans could be rebuilt to serve the people hurt and temporarily displaced by the hurricane and floods. Naomi Klein suggests some ways that could happen in the *Nation* ("Let the People Rebuild New Orleans," 26 September 2005). But even less doubt attaches to this prediction: Katrina enables a very different transformation that would otherwise have been too politically difficult to achieve. New Orleans can now be "renewed" along the gentrification lines favored by its elite and paid for by regressive taxes. That has always been the way of "urban renewal" in the US (with infrequent, minor, and mostly cosmetic concessions to "peoples'" interests when politically required).

A perfect parallel is offered by the tragic history of New Haven, CT. There, it was not a storm but rather a federal interstate highway project that did the trick. The intersection of I-95 and I-91 was constructed in the 1950s in the center of New Haven's densest residential neighborhoods (composed then mostly of white working-class people). Some 30,000 people (out of a total population of 150,000) were thrown out of neighborhoods they had lived in for generations and to which they could not and did not ever return. Had the intersection of I-95 and I-91 been constructed 2-3 miles east or west, only a few dairy cows would have been displaced. Instead, the highway construction—paid for by regressive taxation—accomplished mass displacement and gentrification to suit the New Haven power elite, namely Yale University. Indeed, Yale officials proceeded to draw ever more federal money to "rebuild" and "renew" New Haven to suit Yale (hyped as a "model" urban renewal for the whole US).

That the plan failed, that New Haven is a fiscal basket case (rising regressive property taxes coupled with falling spending for city services) and a social disaster zone (heightened income and wealth differences and tensions exacerbated by mounting ethnic and racial conflicts)—all that is neatly blamed on local politicians and the remaining poorer citizens. Meanwhile, the immediate blocks around Yale bask in a tax-financed gentrification façade aimed to calm the rich parents of Yale students about where their children will be spending four years and to subsidize a few restaurants and boutiques to distract as many as possible from the actual urban reality.

Community actions and alliances, of the sort Naomi Klein extols for New Orleans, will likely do little more than tangentially modify or perhaps delay the basic outcome being planned now for post-flood New Orleans. Rarely has anything more than that been accomplished by such well-intentioned, "community-based" oppositions to urban renewal elsewhere across the US for the last half century.

Only a powerful, unified, and organized political opposition contesting for power could hope to lead an altogether different urban renewal. And that sort of renewal depends on basic social—including class—changes that such an opposition would have to demand and achieve. No other path is available if New Orleans is to have a different future from that of all the other cities, like New Haven, whose "renewals" have been so grossly unjust and in most cases fiscal disasters as well. It is thus not realistic to limit ourselves to community-based oppositions and their demand for active participation in the rebuilding of New Orleans (to which the elite would respond by providing token representation of carefully handpicked "community representatives"). A "realistic" politics of opposition to what is in store for New Orleans would have to go far beyond reformism.

France's Student-Worker Alliance

Paris, 31 March 2006

Students and workers in France have forged a powerful alliance against the government and its neoliberal economic policies. Mass organizations of high school and university students, all three federations of unions, and all left parties are coordinating actions together. This alliance is shaking the French government in ways and to depths not seen since May 1968. The messages that this alliance sends across Europe and beyond are (1) that dismantling of the welfare state has reached its limits and (2) that continuing the dismantling risks provoking mass resistance. The specter of a real opposition to global neoliberal capitalism *in its centers* has materialized. The pseudo oppositions of the social democrats are exposed.

For years, the "socialist leaders" of Europe have profoundly limited their opposition to the roll-back of social services, wages, and job protections. They offered merely to slow its pace. They had been captured by the corporate mantra—imported from the US and UK—that the world economy and global competition required nothing less than "modernization." This bizarre Orwellian term described an actual historic going backward to a pre-World War II kind of capitalism with its extreme inequalities of wealth, income, power, and cultural opportunities. The current movement in France is so powerful that it has, at least for the moment, silenced the usual voices of left accommodation to neoliberalism.

A political bubble is bursting in France. That bubble emerged as the conservatives currently in power—drawn chiefly from top corporate managements—got carried away in a spiraling neoliberal euphoria. In the linear logic of simplistic politics, they kept pushing one deregulation after another, one assault on job security and labor protections after another. The process spun out of control and inflated beyond politically sustainability.

What took French neoliberalism over the edge was a new rule rushed into law (the CPE) by Prime Minister Dominque de

Villepin. It attacked young workers under 26 years of age by allowing employers to fire them without cause for 2 years instead of the previous rule of 6 months. Such a step would save employers more of the costs and bad publicity of justifying dismissals in the special tribunals France established to hear workers' complaints of unjust terminations.

In the inverted language of neoliberal public policy, the French government tried to sell the CPE law as "labor reform sensitive to minority youth needs." Employers would now hire more of the unemployed Arab and African youth—those who had protested their conditions so dramatically last autumn.

French officials tried thus to market a law subsidizing business as if it were meant to provide social support for poor minorities. However, millions of French citizens, including many minority youth, were not fooled. Those are the millions demonstrating in increasing numbers over the last two weeks.

The CPE law is actually more the expression of French politicians seeking support from—and therefore pandering to—the corporations. The law is of little actual interest to corporations in France, however. As reported to the *International Herald Tribune* (24 March 2006), two major employers of French young people were perfectly content with the 6-month period that the CPE law aimed to "reform." The Accor hotel chain and McDonald's and its local restaurant franchisees pointed to their sustained growth and success. McDonald's employs 35,000 with an average age of 22, enjoys better sales in France than in most other countries, and plans to open 30 new restaurants in 2006. In fact, France offers profitable investments because of its rich markets, technological dynamism, employee skills and aptitudes. The particular job protections removed by the CPE law simply matter little even for the firms most dependent on the youth labor market targeted by that law.

Why, then, did French political leaders rush through a law that provided little benefit to employers while it mobilized a powerful alliance of students and workers? The answer is that French politicians took their pandering to neoliberal hype too far in what even many of them now widely recognize as a colossal mistake. Privatizing enterprises and freeing markets from state interventions and regulations had long been proclaimed by business leaders as a "reform that will revitalize the economy." They wanted to make more money. Economists did their usual job of rationalizing and legitimizing these business objectives. Their economic "science" proclaimed such a reform as the entire nation's "best" course of action. In the mutual reinforcement of politicians and economists, they badly overshot the target and produced the dangerous political backlash that is now happening in France.

Something like this is also happening in Germany. But the form it has taken there is not street demonstrations and a massive student-worker alliance. Instead, a new Left Party has emerged with a position parallel to the French opposition to the CPE. Last year's voter defeats of the new neoliberal European constitution in France and the Netherlands have now evolved into a much deeper counter-hegemonic movement. An historic political shift is underway in Europe.

The real question now is whether the student-worker alliance will remain merely an opposition to neoliberalism or whether it will mature into a movement for an alternative to capitalism as the best security against a resumption of neoliberalism. The rest of the world, including the mass of Americans hurt by years of neoliberal policies, have enormous stakes in the answer to that question. If the media in the US were not owned by the supporters of neoliberalism, they would present the historic importance of this question and explore the alternative answers. Instead, they perform their subservient tasks by obscuring the significance of France's student-worker alliance and grossly inflating the tangential vandalisms of a very few and the all-too-predictable provocations of the police.

Lessons of a Left Victory in France

12 April 2006

France's leading bureaucrats, from President Jacques Chirac on down, have been defeated. French neoliberalism—the dismantling of its welfare state in favor of business— has suffered a serious blow. A powerful alliance of high-school and university students and of organized labor achieved the victory against the government's law that undercut job security for workers under 26 years of age.

The alliance forced Chirac to annul the law—exactly what he and the other current leaders had said was absolutely illegal and impossible. Now what matters most is how everyone in France and beyond—business and political conservatives, on one side, and students, labor unions, and the left, on the other side—will understand what has happened. Their different understandings will shape how both sides adjust their respective organizations, strategies, and tactics.

No doubt, the French right and its big business base will try hard to rebuild their organizations and their damaged popular standing. Likewise, they will resume, albeit in other ways, their long-term goal of "reforming" labor laws and conditions to the advantage of business. The lessons they will draw from their defeat is how to avoid any more political defeats along the way. They will need to split the left opposition better than they did this time. They will need to disguise their projects much better as driven by "national" or "economic" or "security" interests that "everyone in France" shares. Big money will be made by the political and business "consultants," "think tanks," and academic "advisors" brought in to repackage the French right's program.

On the other side, the French left and left forces elsewhere facing comparable enemies—that is, the global left—will need to draw the very different lessons from their victory. And the lessons are many. First, a badly disunited left—divided along age, gender, income, immigrant, educational, ethnic, and other lines—found it possible as well as necessary to unite. The unifying focus was on their common relation to the security and conditions of labor. Second, the power of this particular focus undermined the French government's repeated efforts to split the better paid from the less well-paid workers, the immigrant from the non-immigrant, the young from the older, and the more from the less-educated. Third, the government's effort to invoke "the law" as expressing the "democratic will of the people" failed to dissuade a mass movement that believed it represented the people far better and far more genuinely. A kind of dual power situation emerged—a formal versus an informal government—that helped millions of French men and women to see through the formal government's appeals to "national unity." French nationalism failed to overcome the opposition's appeal to the interests of workers and students against the other, different part of French society. The concept of society as a site of struggle between basically opposed social forces became common sense on the left and for the solid majority of French "public opinion" that consistently backed the demonstrators against the government. Finally and perhaps most importantly, the alliance of students and workers confronts the lesson that unified, mass, direct political action can win battles.

The lessons for the French are also lessons for the rest of us. A major battle was won, but the war continues, in France as elsewhere. Businesses will continue to press governments for laws and regulations favoring their needs for profits, rich executive pay packages, and corporate expansion. They will continue to seek advantages in global competition by demanding concessions from workers, consumers, and students. They will pour ever more resources into publicity campaigns, politicians, and "research" that aim to convince people that meeting business needs is what will bring reform, modernization, prosperity, and democracy to everyone. They are gearing up for future battles.

The workers, students, and consumers will face again, in France as elsewhere, the question of whether and how they can unify and mobilize to win those future battles. But sooner or later, they will have to resolve the following key questions that had already been raised during the demonstrations before Chirac accepted defeat and that continue to agitate the student demonstrations on related issues. Do we wait for the next neoliberal attack and fight again to repel it or do we fight this war in another way by challenging the very economic structure that pits employers against employees in endless battles? Might our best strategy be to mobilize all the energy and unity revealed in France this March and April to struggle for a basic change in the organization of production so that workers become their own bosses? Is the cooperative enterprise rather than the capitalist enterprise the way forward to an economic future without endless battles pitting the corporations' alliances against the worker-student-consumer alliances?

A lesson about the US mass media also deserves to be drawn yet again. They mostly ignored the momentous events in France. Some found good copy in wildly exaggerating the scattered violence whose minimal scope and impact actually attested to the mass demonstrations' remarkable organization, discipline, and solidarity. A few took seriously the French government's effort to paint its anti-worker law as motivated by a desire to provide jobs for impoverished immigrant youth whose needs they have systematically ignored. Explicitly or implicitly, most news stories and analyses lectured "the French" on their failure to "modernize" their economy in the neoliberal manner of the US, UK, and other "forward-looking" economies. With few exceptions, the private mass media dutifully did their part to prevent any contagion from the remarkable French spring of 2006.

The Minimum Wage, Labor, and Politics

22 September 2006

The minimum wage tragedy goes beyond the 15 million US workers now earning $5.15 per hour or $206 per forty-hour week before tax and other deductions. It goes beyond the facts that $5.15 was already low when Congress set it in September 1997, and that Congress has since kept it frozen. Meanwhile, living costs rose 26 percent since 1997 (including a medical care rise of 43 percent, a 52-percent increase in child-care and nursery school costs, and a 134 percent increase in gasoline's price). Finally, it goes beyond the low minimum wage's disproportionate impact on single-adult families, women, and ethnic (especially Hispanic) minorities.

The tragedy lies in this: a $5.15 minimum wage in 2006 teaches a lesson about labor and politics in America, but one that remains unlearned by those who need it most. To see this, consider that minimum wages in Britain and France are much higher than in the US and are scheduled to increase again this fall. Workers in those countries relate differently to politics. They demand that politicians, whatever their other foreign and domestic actions, attend to some minimum labor interests. Through their unions or independently, workers there undertake job actions, demonstrate publicly, and vote effectively to punish enemies of labor interests. The British and French minimum wages reflect their workers' political consciousness, militancy, and mobilization.

Battles over the minimum wage have always been political. Workers (not all but most) want higher minimum wages and employers (not all but most) don't. Unlike what happened in Britain (under mostly a labor party government) and France (under mostly a conservative party government), in the US across the last decade, employers won, while labor lost on the minimum wage as on most other labor issues. That loss partly reflected a mistaken political strategy: one focused too much on producing and publicizing "proofs" that the benefits of a higher minimum wage outweighed its costs and too little on mobilizing labor and its friends to defeat its enemies. Labor apparently could not grasp that arguments claiming to know (to have "measured") the benefits and costs of higher or lower minimum wages are illusions no matter which side makes them. Efficiency arguments are self-satisfied hot air pretending to be scientific truth. Nor, as we shall show, can cost-benefit analyses deliver what they claim; they never have.

No doubt, a low minimum wage imposes costs on society, including its recipients and their families (1) physical and mental deterioration because of inadequate nutrition, shelter, medical care, (2) low investment in education and training, (3) damages from living in unclean, unsafe, or violent neighborhoods, (4) damages from dependence on poor public transportation, public emergency room healthcare, and public welfare, unemployment, and family support services, (5) damages from interactions with police, courts, and prisons, (6) damages from poor job benefits (pensions, medical leave allowances, medical insurance, etc.), and so on. Raising the minimum wage would likely reduce the above listed costs plus enhance the consumption, self-esteem, and general well-being for 15 million Americans and their communities. Not surprisingly, labor advocates identify the costs of a higher minimum wage far less comprehensively and measure them differently so that their conclusions find that *the costs of a higher minimum wage are decisively outweighed by its benefits*.

Business advocates basically reverse the argument. The costs and benefits they identify and how they count them "proves" that the costs of raising the minimum wage *outweigh its benefits*. They argue, for example, that employers will fire workers rather than pay higher minimum wages, and that the resulting unemployment will proliferate social costs. They also suggest that raising the minimum wage will contribute to inflation and thus to its many negative social costs.

The cost-benefit calculations of the two sides clash, but do their opposing proofs matter? Are the resources used to make and disseminate such calculations effective in the political battle over the minimum wage? Was that the best possible strategy for labor, or was it mistaken? Because US labor lost that battle repeatedly for a decade, these questions deserve answers.

The first problem with the labor strategy concerns the very idea of identifying and measuring the consequences (positive and negative, "benefits" and "costs") of raising the minimum wage. The difficulty lies in the fact that such consequences are infinite in number, variety, and duration. No one can know, let alone count, *all of them* to prove that the benefits outweigh the costs. All any cost-benefit study ever did was select and count *some of them*. And different calculators with different agendas usually identify and count costs and benefits differently.

Secondly, anything shown to be a consequence of raising the minimum wage is easily shown to be a consequence as well of other factors. For example, when better mental health follows a rise in the minimum wage, the latter cannot be assumed to be the sole cause. Many other factors—known and unknown, present and past—also play their roles. It is no more feasible to identify and measure all the consequences of a changed minimum wage than it is feasible to identify and measure all the factors that combine to produce any of those consequences. Claims to have made such comprehensive identifications and measurements do not deserve to be taken seriously no matter how confidently they are advertised as "scientific."

And they are taken less seriously now than ever in the political battle over the minimum wage. True, the labor and business sides each perform their (partisan) calculations of differently selected costs and benefits to reach their opposite conclusions. Each side appeals to public opinion and to Congress, which sets the minimum wage. But what decides the success of opposing appeals is not either side's calculations and proofs. Those are, after all, complex and not comparable; they also vary depending on the many assumptions of each calculator. Each side finds and exposes flaws in the other's argument;

each side repairs such flaws. The endless changes compound the intricacies to quickly spin beyond the public's or the politicians' interest or attention.

The cost-benefit calculations, to be sure, acquire some limited importance—ironically—only *after* the battle is won by business. Then the business side provides its calculations to its political friends gratis as a convenient cover to disguise their siding with business (minority) against labor (majority). To avoid responsibility for favoring business, those politicians publicize the business calculations as "scientific proof" that the benefits of a frozen minimum wage exceed its costs for everyone, for the whole economy and society. Those politicians then can and do insist that all they did was vote for what is best for everyone, their democratic duty.

What matters in US politics is which side commits the greater resources to persuade, promote, and dazzle their audiences, demonize its opponent, and/or bribe its way to success. It's not either side's calculations or "proofs" but rather the preponderance of public relations that wins the political battle. Because business committed more resources for the last ten years, it froze the minimum wage. To avoid losing, labor would have had either to match or outspend business… or else mobilize its membership to substitute politically effective agitation for such spending.

French Election's Deeper Meaning

20 May 2007

France's presidential election results are deeply contradictory. The victory for the *patronat*—the nation's dominant big business community—may prove extremely dangerous in terms of an enemy reawakened by that victory. The losses for the French left—which still retains the support of half the nation's electorate—may provoke its return to the debate between reform and revolution under conditions strongly favoring the latter as its new policy.

Despite the issues of immigration, crime, and foreign policy that also figured in the results, the French election was remarkable—as has happened often since the French revolution of 1789—in clearly demarcating the basic economic issues. Once again, the key political divisions concerned capitalism and government policy toward capitalist enterprises. In May 2007, the welfare state tradition in France—dating back at least to the popular front policies of Leon Blum in the 1930s—confronted perhaps its strongest political counterattack. Given the Left's inability to promote its message with anything like the resources provided to the Right by its business financiers, the resulting impact on French voters was hardly surprising.

Nicholas Sarkozy, the victor, mocked the accumulated socialist reforms imposed on capitalists in France—its showcase European welfare state—as hopelessly misguided. Those reforms, he insisted, had caused the nation's economic problems. Perpetuating those reforms would mean continued failure to liberate capitalist growth and technical dynamism. Only that liberation—often packaged as "modernizing"—could revive French economic progress; it would ensure, Sarkozy promised, sustainable prosperity.

Vote shifts by French workers who had formerly supported the Left made the difference. They were, to say the least, dissatisfied with the economic conditions in France's welfare state. So they listened to the French Right's heavily promoted argument that those conditions resulted from socialist reforms.

Relentlessly, France's 35-hour work week and generous state welfare programs (5-week paid vacations, national medical care, secure pensions, subsidized childcare) were characterized as wasteful impediments to the economic revival that would flow from "freeing" capitalist entrepreneurship. Removal of counterproductive reforms comprised the "modernization" that a global economy and the European Union required if France was to resume its prosperity, national power, and international prestige. The *patronat* successfully turned many French voters against the welfare state as no longer protecting them. Those voters no longer supported the left parties, who continued to endorse the welfare state.

The socialists split in their reaction to the Right's attacks on the welfare state. Division weakened them politically. Some socialists accepted the Right's arguments. They too would "modernize" France but more gradually and with more care to protect French workers along the way. This position effectively endorsed the Right's view of the welfare state. The other wing of the socialists stuck obstinately to the old reform programs and slogans and simply ignored widespread disaffection among constituents. Many socialists—including the losing Presidential candidate, Ségolène Royal—combined (or vacillated between) both wings. Such socialist ambivalence added to voter disaffection.

Do the French election results, then, represent a clear victory for the Right over the Left? Yes and no. Polling results and also my interviews with a cross-section of the French electorate suggest that Sarkozy's triumph may induce major changes on the Left inside and perhaps outside France as well. Undermining the welfare state may prove to be a short-term gain for capitalism achieved at the cost of a new Left that challenges capitalism far more profoundly than the welfare state and its leftist supporters ever did.

Sarkozy's defeat of the socialists returns the French Left to the old issue of reform versus revolution. Basically, since the Great Depression and through May 1968, the French Left has opted for reform rather than revolution in response to capitalism's crises. It reasoned that revolution would invite an overwhelming and effective crushing of the Left by the forces of "order." It doubted that workers would support a revolutionary program. So the goals were kept within the framework of reforms. Reforms would constrain capitalists in the surpluses they could appropriate from their workers and in what they could do with their surpluses to enhance their profits and competitive positions.

Reforms would return to the workers—in the form of government programs financed by corporate taxes—a portion of the surpluses they had produced for their employers. But the capitalists would be left in the position of appropriators and distributors of the surpluses produced by their productive workers. Occasionally, the private capitalists—those elected by and responsible above all to the shareholders—gave way to government officials appointed to replace them (as in Mitterrand's socialist policies). But those state officials ran the corporations much as the private capitalists had (hence their designation as "state capitalists") and exactly reproduced the private capitalists' appropriation of their workers' produced surpluses. In any case, no revolutionary change occurred; the workers did NOT eject these boards of directors (private or state) to become instead collectively their own boards of directors. The workers remained only workers; the boards of directors remained "others."

The reforms of capitalism won by successive Lefts were accompanied by promises that those reforms would be secure. Reforms were the payoff gained by foregoing the revolution. Now it is clear that welfare state reforms neither were nor are secure. So long as the capitalists retain their positions as corporate boards of directors, they will have both the incentives and the means to undo reforms won by the socialists and social democrats in Europe, by the New Deal and later Democrats in the US, and by the comparable political formations across the world.

The Left proponents of a revolutionary policy against capitalism may now be able to defeat the reformists on the Left by arguing precisely that reforms won cannot be secure so long as capitalists endure. If so, it will have been capitalism's successful rollback of the welfare state that swings the balance within the Left from reform to revolution. The demise of the reformist Left within the socialist, communist, Trotskyist, and other left parties and the emergence of a deeply and widely grounded revolutionary left alternative will then confront capitalism with perhaps the greatest challenge in its history.

Mass Political Withdrawal

20 July 2007

In regular high school rituals, teachers berate students for their disinterest in, mockery of, and/or failure to focus on "the important issues" in elections for student government. Students are forced to hear about cherishing their right to vote, taking the issues seriously, and participating fully. Most never do. Some notice that teachers likewise take little interest in their elections for faculty government either. The explanation: education "administrations" exercise exclusive power over most of what happens in schools.

Teachers and students have very limited powers over very secondary issues. Whether and how they participate in student and teacher politics reflects their reaction to the realities of power inside schools.

Politics in the larger society increasingly resemble this school situation. In the United States as in many other advanced capitalist societies, politics today reflects a deepening mass withdrawal. People increasingly disparage politics and politicians, inform themselves less about political issues, participate less or focus on less general, more narrow issues when they do. A June 12, 2007 *Los Angeles Times* poll showed that a historically very low 27 percent of Americans think that Congress is doing a good job.

The June 10, 2007 French legislative elections saw the largest percentage of eligible voters not bothering to vote in such elections in recent French history. British polls show historically high distaste for parties and for the entire parliamentary "circus." The *Los Angeles Times* poll also showed that the brief spurt of hope in the US after the Democrats won the November 2006 congressional elections had dissipated by June 2007, when once again 73 percent of Americans bemoan the US Congress for doing "business as usual"—a very negative judgment.

Interest and participation in civic affairs including politics has been declining since the mid-1970s, as Robert D. Putnam's

2000 bestseller, *Bowling Alone*, documents about the US. The evidence suggests that withdrawal from politics is also a transnational phenomenon. Indeed, it is part of neoliberal globalization. As the ruling policies and ideas advocated and the ruling policies implemented a reduced role for the state, mass political engagement shrank.

The last quarter century has seen the greater or lesser undoing of welfare states in countries across the world. Those welfare states had been established to dig those countries out of the Great Depression, World War II, and their social consequences. Governments suddenly became much more massively involved in caring for people than ever before. Beyond unemployment insurance, Social Security, and government jobs, a widespread feeling arose that governments could, should, and would serve peoples' basic needs. Starting in the disastrous 1930s, politicians did not merely *talk* about government serving the people. The government actually did so in dramatic, unprecedented ways. The general public then could and did see the point in political engagement: learning about candidates, parties, and platforms, following the relationships between promises made and kept, participating in meetings, organizing, campaigning, and voting.

Since the mid-1970s, the decline of welfare states—neoliberal privatization and deregulation—produced two hardly surprising results: (1) ever fewer people received public services and (2) their contacts with a public sector increasingly pinched for resources yielded disappointment, disgust, and disengagement. Political efforts to stop or reverse this flow of events were repeatedly insufficient. The mass of people witnessed this. They have felt less and less interested in or related to politics as government retreated from the quality and quantity of the basic services it had provided to the people since the 1930s. Had its enemies responded to neoliberalism by effectively mobilizing mass confrontation against neoliberalism's financiers and supporters, contemporary politics might have taken quite a different turn. But that has not—or at least not yet—happened.

This broken relationship between the mass of people and politics takes many forms. Abstention from voting is only one of the reactions when the basic issues of life (jobs, personal security, health, housing, etc.) are ever less objects of effective state activity. For those who maintain some involvement in politics, they focus on different issues—in the US, access to firearms, immigration, abortion, global warming, homosexuality, and so on.

Because so many of today's shrunken mass of voters fixate on such issues, commentators mistakenly infer that those have become "the more important" to voters. An alternative interpretation holds that the basic issues of life remain as important as always but neoliberalism has increasingly taken them out of the government's realm of activity. The state is blocked ideologically and practically from attending to them since they are "better left to the private free market." Thus, mass interest in politics correspondingly reduces to the issues around which state policies still matter, e.g. gun control, homosexual marriage, abortion, pollution controls, etc.

Those mobilized by and around such issues stay in politics. The rest of the population loses interest in politics or perhaps votes for those candidates whose take on such issues they share. Increasingly, voters are only casually and momentarily involved by the crescendo of TV ads preceding elections. Hence candidates must raise millions to buy the ads without which they cannot win. One week after the election, few remember or care much.

This situation afflicts all political parties: both those perceived to have engineered the welfare state's demise and those perceived to have failed to stop it. Their constituents are ever less engaged or involved. Politics reverts to little more than the machinations of tiny political apparatuses composed mostly of the elected officials for whom politics and personal career are identical. The "political struggle" becomes chiefly one in which those apparatuses compete for contributions—largely from the same sources among businesses and the richest individuals. The latter correspondingly gain ever greater influence. For the rest of us, politics is a spectator sport suffering declining interest and attendance.

So long as those victimized by neoliberalism respond with political withdrawal, neoliberal politicians will keep smiling while reciting the usual homilies for democracy (like the school teachers). They will scold non-voters while insisting that their votes would not have changed the outcomes (quite the encouragement to vote!). They will stay focused on fund-raising from neoliberalism's chief beneficiaries to keep themselves in power.

The key question: can neoliberalism's enemies find ways to convert a withdrawal from politics into a serious challenge to the social forces that undercut the post-1930s welfare states?

Capitalism Crashes, Politics Changes

26 October 2008

This widening and deepening economic crisis is transforming US politics. New possibilities are emerging for activists if they can see and respond creatively to them.

One possibility follows from rethinking the Obama candidacy in the light of recent German politics. Obama has already garnered an historically disproportionate share of the campaign contributions of the US business leadership. The next president will arrive at an historic moment when most of the business leadership will be looking to (if not also begging) Washington for massive intervention to save the private capitalist economy. These conditions may then ripen a major realignment within US politics.

The economic crisis is further straining the already stressed Republican alliance between traditionally conservative business and libertarian interests, on the one hand, and the small business and religious groups, on the other. McCain's political difficulties and attempts to solve them—for example, the Palin choice—provide further evidence. Pressed by mounting business needs for massive government help, a sizeable portion of the Republican Party may be ready for a "grand coalition" to govern the country with a sizeable portion of the Democrats.

The centrist Democrats gathered around the Clintons and also Obama may well see the political possibilities of splitting the Republicans in this way. Such a grand coalition with the Republicans could control both the executive and legislative branches (and thus, within a very few years, also the judicial). Such a grand coalition would be uniquely capable of undertaking the difficult and costly interventions required to manage the economic crisis and its dangerous political and cultural consequences at home and abroad. Both components of such a coalition might see it and its task of crisis management as politically inevitable no matter how unpopular. This might be an attractive prospect for major portions of both parties.

Recent German politics offers an obvious, instructional parallel because there a similar "grand coalition" now governs Europe's most powerful economy. Another kind of crisis in Germany provoked its grand coalition. Some years ago, Germany's social democratic commitments (a regulated capitalism with workers' protections and social welfare programs such as socialized medicine, generous pensions, subsidized education, etc.) clashed with the neoliberal demands of its leading capitalists. They wanted to compete more profitably both within the European Economic Community and globally. They resented the competitive advantages of US and UK firms whose governments (since Reagan and Thatcher) had rolled back earlier regulations on corporations and social programs.

Pushing the two major German parties—Christian Democrats and Social Democrats—proved insufficient for German business interests. Too many constituencies inside both parties opposed those interests' neoliberalism. The end result was a stalemated German politics. Its resolution was an explicit, formal "grand coalition." The two parties agreed to share governing power. It was clear that this coalition could and would pursue a neoliberal rollback of Germany's social welfare system (although likely more slowly than in the US and UK). Germany's grand coalition aimed to overcome what its supporters saw as an economic crisis: German global competitiveness subverted by costly state regulation of business and taxes used for social welfare programs.

A similar grand coalition in the US could likewise be packaged as necessary to manage an economic crisis threatening the entire society. This US election and its interaction with the capitalist crash have produced many of the preconditions for such a result.

Germany's grand coalition provoked unexpected consequences that raise intriguing possibilities for the US as well. The most arresting consequence was the development of a new left political party, *Die Linke* ("the Left" in German). It was formed by a merger of two political groups: (1) the left wing of the Social Democrats who opposed the party's grand coalition strategy, and (2) the successor party to the former communist party of East Germany. *Die Linke* has been growing very quickly and receiving much larger votes than was expected in both regional and national elections. With proportional representation, *Die Linke* won a significant number of seats in both the national and some regional parliaments. It takes positions clearly and explicitly to the left of the grand coalition and thus of that coalition's Social Democratic component.

Die Linke is thus now *the* left opposition to German neoliberalism. It has been drawing massive voter support away from the grand coalition's Social Democrats whom it easily portrays as having abandoned Germany's working classes. Yet, *Die Linke* confronts the problem of what alternative program to offer. After all, the Social Democratic Party may leave the grand coalition and resume its historic role as the regulator of business and the protector of state social programs. This would leave the far smaller *Die Linke* with no distinctive political identity and at the mercy of Social Democratic Party decisions. The key issue for *Die Linke* thus has become what new left program it can devise and effectively project to keep attracting voters, especially the young, and to chart a new direction for Germany different from the traditional Social Democratic notions of state intervention.

Something similar may visit US politics. If a grand coalition forms in the US, perhaps the left wing of the Democratic Party might find that unacceptable. Perhaps some trade unions would finally decide that their relentless decline while allied with the Democrats would only be accelerated by becoming very junior partners in such a grand coalition. Perhaps such breakaways from the Democrats and from traditional union politics would need and even want to build a new left party with the large but largely unorganized left constituencies across the US. And like *Die Linke*, a new left party in the US would need to develop a new program different from the conventional "US liberalism."

Politics always mixes representations of what exists now, what could exist, and what should exist. Not the least influence on the future of US politics will be the conceptions of possible futures we can now glimpse, debate, and pursue. Those on the political Right may find the grand coalition described above a goad toward developing new right parties. That only strengthens the case for new political thinking and action on the Left.

INDEX